Observations of a Drifter

Vol II

Tennessee to New Jersey

Matthew Bryant Parham

Vol II

This manuscript is an ongoing and constantly evolving work, one that I slowly add to as the years go on. Each time I make a significant addition or add more stories, I release the entirety of the work as a new volume. This particular work, Vol II, contains new stories and observations as well as all the material from the previous volume. This is done so that, if you buy the latest work, you are not missing anything from the past.

For previous readers, you can find a directory on page 284 to specifically guide you to the new content.

For all others, I hope you find this book both entertaining and helpful.

Vol II

The Beginning

For years, I have traveled. Walking different shoes, observing and recording the world around me and how my mind functioned within that world.

The idea being to record and understand every aspect of the mind; All its inner workings; Its emotions, desires, reactions to things. Understand all forms of turmoil and quell them. Over the years, I have faced down, understood, and quelled every bit of turmoil I could find, often seeking out hardships or throwing myself into new, unusual situations, trying to find/trigger some new sort of turmoil that I could understand and quell. The concept being similar to that of a vaccine; If I find it now, understand it and quell it, I will not be susceptible to it in the future. So I push and seek out struggles.

I generally go from town to town, city to city. Sometimes with money, often times with none. I travel almost exclusively by foot, though I have occasionally switched to bus, bike, hitchhiking, and rental cars. I have accumulated a lot of stories along the way, some of them quite wild.

The story is still ongoing, of course. A constant excursion and adventure.

In this book, I will share stories and quips from my travels, along with excerpts from the notebook of observations that I have been building for the past seven years.

As a preface, I would like to thank all the wonderful people that I have met along the way in these journeys. The ones that are not mentioned in these stories, but who are very dear to me. All the acts of kindness and hospitality. I very rarely use names in my works, but you know who you are, and so do I.

Vol II

Stories from Volume One:

Arizona to New York State

(Adventure, Love, Near-Death, Trouble)

This particular story begins at the end of my stay in Tucson, Arizona. I had come to Tucson on a Greyhound with $20 in my pocket and a backpack on my shoulders. The idea being to live on the streets and experience the city's grit. While there, I would meet and befriend drifters, the homeless, gang members, drug addicts.

I would have many experiences, both pleasant and unpleasant; Even facing death at one point while sitting on a bus stop bench. Having become too complacent in the city, too relaxed, I let my guard down and my awareness slip.

Sitting there, with a 40-lb backpack strapped to my back, watching traffic go by, a 20-year-old Hispanic fellow jumped off a bicycle with a knife in his hand, placing it to my throat before I could react.

As he stood there, crazed and shouting gibberish, I was resigned to the fact that this might not end well for me. But, I remained calm and waited for an opening.

Someone from the parking lot behind us yelled in our direction, causing the fellow with the knife to look up. Seizing the opportunity, I grabbed his wrist, pushed the knife away, and jumped up. He looked pretty squirmy, and with a 40-lb bag on my back, I decided to jump backwards, put space between us, and pull out my knife.

He took a wild swing as I unstrapped and threw off my backpack. I squared up with him, preparing to face whatever happened next, when someone yelled that they were calling the police. The fellow looked at them, looked at me, then scampered off.

I stood there for a moment, processing the events. Had the fight commenced, it would have been an awful ordeal. Whether I clipped him or he clipped me, either way, it would have been unfortunate.

Only a few days later, the memories of the knife encounter still fresh in my mind, I had an unbelievably pleasant and uplifting experience.

By this point, I had been in the city for a while, scraping along and bartering for things I needed.

While enjoyable, I was beginning to get a bit bored with it, so I decided to hit the local day labor.

Unfortunately, when I checked my pockets for ID, I discovered mine was missing. It was nowhere to be found. I had spent the last few days traversing all corners of the city, so retracing my steps would be a massive ordeal. I would literally have to search the entire city of Tucson. It was in that moment that I did something I generally did not do at the time. I looked up at the sky and began to pray to the Lord.

While I did tend to frequent religious sermons and speeches, I wasn't particularly religious myself. I had always listened to the sermons and speeches for the metaphors, never actually considering the doctrine as truth. But, in that moment, I looked up and made a sincere plea and offer. If my ID were to make it back to me somehow, I said, I would take that as a motivating factor to frequently read the Word and sincerely give it a chance. I couldn't promise that I would be swayed or that I would begin to believe, but I would give it an honest opportunity to strike me.

 After making that plea, I took a look at my watch. On a whim, I decided to head to the downtown library to check my messages for the day. I arrived 15 minutes before closing time, quickly signed up for a computer, and sat down. Five minutes before the library was to close, a gentleman sat down next to me, having been randomly assigned to that computer.   He took a look at me.

With a cheerful smile, he said "I think I have something that belongs to you".

He pulled out his wallet and handed my ID to me.

"I found this in an alleyway near the University. I saw you downtown a few weeks back, standing with a group of transients, so I recognized your face on the ID and picked it up. But I figured you weren't going to be getting it because I'm scheduled to leave town tomorrow."

Astonished and bewildered, a big smile came across my face.

That's when he said, "I must be your Guardian Angel."

I shook the fellow's hand and thanked him. He wouldn't tell me his name, only wishing me luck on my travels.

True to my word, I now carry a Bible with me everywhere I go.

With my ID in hand, I signed up for the day labor, gaining an easy opportunity to make money. Incidentally, this would lead to my departure from Tucson, sending me further along my path.

It occurred early in the morning; I received a phone call from the day labor, asking me if I was interested in taking an out-of-town assignment. It was 7 days a week, 12 hours a day, they said. Lodging, transportation, and a daily food allowance was included.

I was pretty content in the city and wasn't ready to depart just yet, but this sounded like the beginnings of an adventure. A unique experience.

So I accepted.

I spent the day getting my affairs in order. Walking to different parts of the city, selling a few items, repaying small debts. As the sun began to set, I opened up my map and set out towards the day labor across town.

I walked all through the night, mile after mile in the cold, feet bloodied and raw from my worn-out boots, racing the clock, looking for Palo Verde Road.

Daylight was nearing by the time I arrived and sat down next to the building. I could hear someone near the dumpsters, digging around, a sound I had become accustomed to in the city. I took off my boots and wrapped my feet, preparing for the adventure that lay ahead.

5 am rolled around, a van pulled up to the back of the building and unlocked the door. I went inside, along with six other fellows. They handed each of us a hardhat, gloves, and $100. We hopped in the van and headed off to a new town, where work and lodging awaited us.

It turned out to be gritty work, cleaning a power plant from top to bottom with hydroblast guns, fire hoses, and chisels. Crawling into nooks and crannies, hanging onto ropes and ladders. It was an odd assortment of employees, too. There were maybe 30 of us. A diverse gathering of the homeless and downtrodden from the streets of Tucson. Hard-working homeless and downtrodden.

I enjoyed the new surroundings, the small desert town. Going to work during the day and having a bed to sleep in at night. I was excelling at the work, too. Though it almost killed me.

It was the third week on the job. We had made our way halfway down the plant, using hydroblast guns to cut huge slabs of lime off the interior of the furnace walls, letting the rock and water drain into a huge bowl below, out a horizontal pipe. When that pipe clogged, they sent me outside to clear it.

I spent all day crawling, mining my way through the pipe. Chipping away at the rock with a small, sawed-off shovel, pushing the rock and sludge out with my feet as I went. Until, finally, I reached the end. I could see markings that indicated the spot where the pipe forked up at a 90-degree angle into the giant bowl above.

Thinking all was well, unaware that they had continued to use the hydroblast guns while I was mining, filling the bowl above me full of water, I hammered away at the remaining rock.

After several minutes, a small chunk finally broke loose. That's when I noticed the whole thing starting to buckle. I instinctively flipped over onto my back, and, in a flash, the remaining rock crumbled and I was shot to the other end of the pipe by a river of water and rock.

I slammed into a metal ridge at the end of the pipe, one of my legs sticking out of the horizontal opening and the rest of my body being pulled down a vertical opening that led into another pipe.

I remember observing the river of water flowing

over me, coming from behind me. The immense amount of pressure pushing down on my torso, pushing my hardhat-covered head into my chest, pushing me down the vertical opening.

I didn't know it at the time, but outside the horizontal opening, one of my coworkers had a hold of my leg, likely saving me from getting pulled into the vertical opening. He held onto my leg despite the river of water and rock, leading to a good gash on his hand.

When the water finally subsided, I could see daylight and hear people shouting. I was pulled out of the pipe by my coworker.

He and I had our share of disagreements in the past. We were always cordial, but we didn't exactly excel at working together. But his reflex and selfless act in that moment, I'll never forget When it came down to it, he stood up and took action. Standing outside the pipe afterwards, adrenaline still flowing, he kept repeating to me, "I wasn't going to let you go, man, I wasn't going to let you go."

I escaped the ordeal with only minor injuries and was back working within a couple of weeks. Things went smoothly, work went well. I was even hired on as a full-time employee with the company. However... I ended up getting into a bit of trouble.

After 6 weeks of working 12-hour days, 7 days a week, getting off work after hours in a town with not much going on, I began to get a bit restless.

Stopping at one of the local stores, I struck up a conversation with a cashier. A young, pretty Hispanic girl. We hit it off quite well, but I knew I wouldn't have the time to cultivate anything or put energy into dating.

So, with clouded judgment, I slipped her a note and walked out. Now, I'm not saying I solicited her, but I DID mention that I was in town on a work assignment... that I had $800... that I was staying in a nearby hotel, and that I would be there at 7 PM.

Well, 7 PM rolled around and there was a knock at the door.

I opened it to find a cute Hispanic girl, but not the one I was expecting. This one had a police uniform on.

She looked at me and smiled, sweetly uttering "Do you know why I'm here?"

I looked at her, then looked back at the bed, money sprawled across it. "Why are you here?"

She was very sweet, calmly explaining that this sort of thing didn't fly in a small town like this. Apparently, this wasn't the first time this had happened with an out-of-town worker.

In any event, this ended my stint with my employer. I was once again a free man, looking off towards the horizons.

I checked out of the hotel the next day and headed off towards the town, going into all the restaurants, museums, and shops. Being a hedonist and taking it all in. Getting one last hurrah before possibly heading out of town.

As the sun began to set, I spotted a movie theater. A good end to the day, I thought. I went in and bought a ticket and paid for popcorn. Moments later, a dreadfully cute girl strolled up to the counter with the popcorn, with a shy smile on her face, her cheeks blushing, her eyes glistening.

As I took the popcorn, I looked at her, and innocently quipped, "I would ask you to join me, but I'm sure you've already seen them all."

I took the popcorn into the theater and sat down. As the previews began to roll, the girl appeared and sat down next to me. We hit it off instantly. So much so that we left five minutes into the movie, unable to contain our talking.

We hopped into her car and headed into town, stopping at the local diner. At this time, I had $1800 or so shoved into my pockets. We ordered ice cream and sat in one of the booths. Talking, laughing, we never even touched our ice cream.

I knew, inevitably, that I was going to move on, but I couldn't help but be drawn in by this girl. We would end up sharing a lot of exhilarating moments together, building memories and a strong bond over things I thought I would never bond with anyone over. Even now, I still have a fondness for that girl. I am grateful for the time we had and those memories ingrained in my brain. I often replay them on the road, bringing a smile to my face.

I ended up spending a total of three more months in Willcox, spending a month in a hotel before reverting to backpack living, where I would venture into the desert at night and head back into town during the day.

My time in Willcox, was fairly interesting and eventful. Walking around as I do, I developed a relationship with the community, getting to know all its different groups. Befriending the Sheriff, the local police, the shop owners, the youth.

I joined the Mormon Church, learning about their beliefs and way of life, joining the missionaries on door-to-door visits. I also took a job at the local truckstop, meeting a lot of interesting characters passing through from the interstate.

It was a nice town, one that I could see myself settling into. But, as always, adventure kept calling. The need for progression. More stories, more experiences.

I began to plan my next move, considering taking a bus to San Francisco and living on the streets there. But, before that could materialize, the Universe sent another opportunity my way, adding a twist to the story in the form of a unique character.

It took place while I was on shift at the truckstop; I was patching a leak in one of the restrooms when a rather tall fellow came in wearing shorts, a shirt, and a boonie hat. He had a cane in one hand and a large bowie knife on his hip   He seemed vibrant, but a bit off. Like an upbeat, energetic Chevy Chase.

He said he and his girlfriend were travelling across the country and were looking to buy a good off-road vehicle. He said he was willing to overpay and would give me a small finder's fee.

I didn't know of any, but spent a few minutes talking to him anyway, as I did with most interesting characters that came through the door.

We hit it off pretty well and he invited me to smoke marijuana with him and his girlfriend outside. I declined, figuring it wasn't a smart idea, but said I wouldn't mind talking a bit more.

After patching the leak, I headed up front to take lunch. The fellow was outside, sitting at one of the tables. He had a bag of bottled waters and food, saying he found a recently-used illegal- immigrant camp spot in the brush behind the parking lot. He said we could drop it off for the illegals and smoke the marijuana back there, if I didn't want to be seen by my employers or the customers.

Alarms went off a bit. If someone were going to try to kill or rob you, this would be one way of going about it. But I didn't much care. I was a bit bored and had a firearm concealed at my waist.

I walked across the parking lot with him, staying a couple of steps behind for good measure.

He said he was medically retired from the Army, having been a Cavalry Scout, serving in the initial invasion of Iraq. He was rich, he said, and travelled the country looking for interesting things to do. Also taking time for scenic photography, gathering rocks and minerals, and capturing and reselling animals.

This all seemed pretty interesting. I asked a few questions, to test out his knowledge on a few of his claims and to get a glimpse into his perspective.

We arrived at the immigrant camp spot and dropped off the supplies, maybe 20 feet into the desert. We covered it with a small cloth and he etched his "call sign" into the dirt.

At this time, I could hear the cashiers calling my name over the loudspeakers at the truckstop. It sounded pretty urgent, but I couldn't leave without asking a few more questions.

He produced the marijuana, and we began to talk. I told him a bit about the adventures I had been on, the places I had been and the people I had met. I told of my time in the desert and how, even now, I still ventured into the brush to sleep at night

That's when he offered to bring me along with him. Pay me to help collect animals and rocks, help shoulder the gear when climbing hills and mountains.   He said he would teach whatever survival and combat skills I didn't already know and pay for all food/lodging expenses.

I mulled it over for a moment.   I was OK with the possibility of ending up stranded somewhere. I was prepared to fight if this fellow turned out to be a deviant.   I had nothing to lose by leaving; I was already on my way out of the area, considering hopping on a bus. So, I accepted.

He said to gather my things and meet him at a local hotel in an hour to head out.

As we began to head back towards the parking lot, two large Tarantulas emerged from the brush in front of us. They came from opposite directions, heading towards each other. We each grabbed a container off the ground and carefully scooped them up. He handed me $20 and said he could sell them for a decent profit. This is starting off well, I thought.

We spent about a month on the road, hitting different destinations. Exploring the hills and climbing rock faces in Tombstone, monkeying around in the Grand Canyon, hitting all sorts of small towns, exploring off-the-wall shops, restaurants. Heading through Utah, Colorado, Iowa, Kansas, Nebraska. Roving the backroads, stopping to climb giant hills and formations, collecting chunks of rock and minerals.

It was a wild time, certainly, and it didn't seem like it would end anytime soon. The plan was for the three of us to head to New York, gather up a few of his belongings, then head back to Colorado, buy a house, and start a business. Unfortunately, we never made it to New York…

We had been traveling all day and night, making our way towards New York. Following the direction of the GPS, which led us on to Michigan into Detroit.

It was night time, a bit chilly. I remember looking over the smog-filled, uninviting, barren concrete jungle and thinking to myself "I would hate to get stranded here."

Traveling along the interstate, the GPS directed us to exit. We took the exit, being greeted by a large sign:

"Bridge to Canada"

"No return from this point"

Hmm…

I was without my passport, my license; any valid ID. My friend had marijuana on him, and the car was filled with swords, lead balls, black powder, spears. All innocently-collected antiques and novelty items, but not something you want to take to a border crossing.

We pulled into a small parking lot next to the road.   There were two gas pumps and an office of some sort. It was the middle of the night, the whole area was vacant and quiet. Straight ahead were the tolls, leading to the actual bridge.

My friend went inside the office and explained the situation, how we took the exit by mistake. The officer inside told him to speak to a toll operator for instructions. The toll operator seemed unsure of what to do, but told us to go onto the bridge, tell the Canadian toll operators, and they would authorize us to turn around, escorting us back to the US mainland.

We crossed the bridge, giant Canadian flags hanging above, and reached the Canadian tolls. We explained the situation.

After a few moments of hesitation, the officer told us to pull into a secondary area.

Five officers appeared and ordered us out of the Jeep.

That's when they opened the doors and began to search the vehicle, immediately discovering a firearm under the driver's seat. They ordered us to turn around and face the vehicle, pulling out handcuffs.

We had two firearms in the vehicle, both registered and legal, but since we had technically crossed an international border without declaring them, they considered it to be smuggling. The spears, swords, marijuana, and war memorabilia in the back wasn't likely to help matters, either.

I remember the moment we were being handcuffed. My friend planting his head on the hood in disgust, knowing how serious of a moment this had become. This wasn't small potatoes. All our plans had now been derailed.

It's funny, though. I remember viewing the event with indifference. Viewing it as just another twist, another story. Actually looking forward to going along for the ride. It was exciting. It was interesting.

I spent the night in a holding cell and was interviewed by one of the detectives. Satisfied that I wasn't a terrorist or a drug runner, they ended up letting me go. They did, however, seize my firearm, the vehicle, everything in it, and charge my friend with possession of unlawful goods and smuggling. I assumed he must have claimed everything as his, knowing he had the resources to pay fines and hire a good attorney.

In any event, they gave me the dog and bearded dragon we had with us, put me at the border in Detroit, and wished me luck. With no ID, no money, no weapons, no phone, and no friends in the area, I took a good luck at the city in front of me, took a deep breath, and set out on my way.

I was no stranger to surviving in big cities, gathering resources and clawing my way up, but I had never done so while also caring for animals.

I decided I needed to get things rolling quickly, so I headed off into the city.

It was a strange world. The buildings were crumbling, graffiti littered the roads and walls, even on the abandoned cars on the street. Grass was growing wild. It was... post-apocalyptic. I found a couple of pieces of plastic on the ground and fashioned them into shanks, then began to look for a Mormon Church, figuring I could use it as a place to have a replacement ID and debit card mailed.

With no luck that day, I ducked out into a set of bushes next to a fence for the night. It was in a shady neighborhood with houses just on the other side of the fence.

I spent most of the night keeping mosquitoes off the dog. He seemed to understand the situation and our surroundings, keeping quiet and not barking. Occasionally, there would be yelling or loud noises. He would look up, then look at me. I put my hand on his shoulder and he would lay his head back down.

The next day, I managed to contact one of the churches and received directions. I spent the day traversing neighborhoods, alleyways, and parks, finally reaching the church at dusk.

The church grounds were surrounded by a giant fence, almost resembling a prison. Inside, I could see the city's missionaries, all six of them. To their great credit, they had gathered together, preparing to head out and look for me. They handed me a gallon of water and said there was a church service the next day and that I could speak to the Bishop about receiving mail.

 A bit relieved, and tired, I waited until the missionaries left, then scaled the fence, pushing the dog through a small opening down below. I found a nice corner behind the building and the two of us napped.

That morning, I woke up early and made my way back over the fence, waiting for everyone to arrive for the service. I ended up speaking to the Bishop of the church who, to my grateful astonishment, offered to pay for a bus ticket out of the city and provide a good home for the dog. He even paid for a hotel and fast food meal for the night.

 At sunrise the next morning, I made my way to

the Greyhound station and hopped on a bus to Tennessee.

 On arrival, I reacquired my IDs and debit card, then headed to my brother's house in Kentucky. Spending three weeks there, recouping, before getting a call; My buddy had been released and was back in New York. He was told I had made my way south, and was on his way down to pick me up. Unfortunately, he never made it past the New York border.

 As it turned out, he was mentally ill, suffering mania due to a war injury. And, as a result of a mix-up with his debit card, he had been picked up by the police and placed into a mental hospital.

 I hopped onto a bus and headed for New York,

ultimately arriving in Erie, Pennsylvania and using a string of local buses and taxis to make it to Jamestown, where he was being held.

I arrived in Jamestown in the middle of the night. I had the driver drop me off a couple of blocks away from the hospital, where I began to look for a place to sleep. The only covered areas were exceptionally steep, tree-covered hills, nearly 45-degree angles. Tired, I climbed up into one of the hills and laid down, pinning my body between two trees to keep me from sliding down.

I awoke the next morning at sunrise, cleaned myself off a bit and began to head for the hospital, finding a place to stash my knives and mace along the way.

I arrived, showed my ID to the guards, and was directed to the third floor. I stepped off the elevator, was let through a buzzer operated door, and was greeted by the nurses. My friend was eating lunch in a large room, listening to rock music on the radio. There were games and books everywhere. It was actually sort of nice.

For over a week, I visited, spending my days at the hospital and my nights on the steep hill. It soon became apparent that they had no intention of releasing him, even denying his request to be transferred to a VA Hospital. That's when he began to talk of... escaping.

I dutifully presented the option of not attempting an escape, to give a platform to reason, but it was not to be. He wanted out and I was the only one who could help. We spent a few hours talking about it, coming up with a plan. There were several security guards and cameras throughout the hospital, but there was a hole in the security. An unlocked, unguarded exit on the south side of the second floor. A quick bolt could get us out.

I left the hospital and spent the rest of the day scouting the layout of the town. The plan was to head south, towards the Pennsylvania line. I followed the roads, taking note of residential layouts, wooded areas, proximity to police patrols and commercial areas.

With a route set, we were ready. I staged supplies along the route, then headed for the hospital.

I went inside, walked up to the door, and pressed the buzzer. The nurse recognized me and buzzed the door open. I held it wide open and my friend bolted past me, down the stairs. The nurses came running, but I shoved the door closed and hopped down the stairs. He followed me as we ran towards the south exit in full sprint.

Pushing the door open, we took off down the hill onto the residential streets. After 250 yards, his energy started waning. At his current speed, I could see we weren't going to make it to the woods quickly enough, so I diverted, ducking us into a series of backyards, eventually hitting woods and making our way towards the south end of town.

Unfortunately, much to my dismay, he decided he wanted to start walking on the road. We weren't yet out of town, and I knew we wouldn't exactly blend in. He had no shoes, long hair, and his clothes were dirty from the woods. I had on a large camouflage trench coat, was soaking wet from a recent rainstorm, and had leaves stuck in my hair.

  As expected, within a few minutes of walking on the road, we were passed by a patrol car, which stopped and questioned us, quickly discovering who we were. They took him back to the hospital and let me go.

 From there, I headed on, as I do, leaving Jamestown. I haven't spoken to my buddy since our separation.

 He was fooling around with one of the other patients in the hospital. The nurses didn't know. It was comical to see them sneaking around, going into the restroom right behind one of the nurses.

There was an extremely cute girl as a patient. She had dark, shark-like eyes and was on antipsychotics, but she and I hit it off quite well. I would have been willing to marry her, circumstances permitting.

I liked those stress balls. With the happy faces on them.

Vol II

Seattle to San Diego
(Oregon, Matt and the Cat, Death Valley)

This story begins after a 2-month journey from Seattle, having walked to Tacoma, then Castle Rock, hitching a ride to Portland, and making my way out to the Oregon coast. I headed down, hoofing Highway 101 by day and ducked off into the woods and beaches at night, nestling down with my usual tarp and blanket. I had my sights ultimately set on San Diego, but was soon entranced by a small town near the Oregon/California border. Gold Beach.

I had initially arrived in Gold Beach looking for work. Tired and a bit malnourished, I rendezvoused with a fellow I had met a few towns back who had offered to bring me in on a short construction job. A bicyclist, he roamed the coast year-round doing carpentry and stonework. Unfortunately, by the time I arrived in town, the job had ended.

Undeterred, I decided to set up shop in the town anyway. I slept in a grassy area near the river at night, I spent my days roaming the roads, collecting stray cans and containers, taking them to town and turning them in for the recycling deposit.

I soon became enamored by the tranquility of the area. A quiet, friendly beach town, sitting at the base of a bordering mountain wilderness. All its businesses on one stretch of road.

It was my third week in Gold Beach when I met a

couple that was staying on a nearby gravel bar in their motorhome. They had seen me walking around town and thought it would be interesting to hear of my stories, so they offered to pitch a tent for me next to their motorhome.

They were stocked full of food, music, and alcohol. For several weeks, we had an enjoyable time; Sharing stories, enjoying music by the river. They even offered to restock my gear and provide a few days of employment pouring concrete.

However, as usual, a series of unexpected events led to adventure.

One day, on a return stroll from town, a fellow in a dusty green truck pulled over and offered to give me a ride. After a short conversation, he said he had a remote camp up in the mountains where he was dredging the creeks for gold. He liked my story and asked if I would like to help him out with the dredges for a few days.

 I accepted.

 We stopped at my friends' campsite to grab a few light items and leave a note, then headed up to the mountains.

 We spent days exploring the wilderness creeks, traversing boulders and fallen trees, navigating rock slides, looking for signs of gold.

 On the fourth day, back at the mountain camp, the truck lost power and wouldn't start. Being accustomed to walking, I volunteered to hike the 20 miles back to town and send help.

After eight hours of travelling, cutting through the woods and making my way down the winding trails and roads, I finally arrived in town and made the phone call for Dave, sending help.

At that point, I decided to head back to the gravel bar to rendezvous with my friends.

Shortly after setting out, I heard a wailing noise coming from the other side of the highway. There, on the grassy hill, was a kitten, stranded, frightened by the traffic. I went over and sat down next to it, feeding it a bit of food, then standing up and motioning for it to follow me.

I didn't really have the resources to take care of a kitten, nor did it fit with my current plans... But it was stranded and alone, and I wasn't going to leave it. I figured I could take care of it and keep it safe long enough to find it a home.

So, the two of us set off down the road, making our way towards the gravel bar, the cat walking beside me dutifully, like a dog.

We arrived at the gravel bar and began to search for the campsite in the darkness. As I walked around, looking for familiar sights, I began to notice that there were no motorhomes or vehicles in the area at all. It seemed abandoned.

My fears were realized when we approached the river. I clearly recognized this section of the bank, the trees growing nearby. This was the campsite... but there was absolutely nothing there. My friends, the motorhome, the tent, all my gear. It wasn't there.

There we were, the kitten and I. Alone, in the cold. No gear. No resources. And, to complicate things, I could see lightning in the distance, seemingly headed towards us.

With no rain gear or blankets, we needed shelter. The kitten and I headed over to two giant tree trunks lying on the gravel bar. There was enough room between them for us to comfortably squeeze in and lie down. I tore the bark off the trunks and used it to fashion a roof and doorway, packing it with grass and mud to keep rainwater from seeping through.

After an hour or so of work, our shelter was complete. We climbed in and laid down, enjoying the warmth that was building. We would rest easy tonight and regroup tomorrow.

We ended up acquiring a tent and moving to a sand bar near the ocean. I would go out and collect blackberries during the day, selling them and acquiring food for the kitten while he roamed the beach. I would come back at dusk, summon him by playing a song on the flute, then the two of us would eat and fall asleep in the tent.

We rested well there, staying for 3 weeks before finally locating a home for him. Happy with his new surroundings, I bid my little friend farewell and set my sights on the next town.

Just about that time, I was contacted by Dave. He said he was headed down to southern Nevada and wondered if I wanted to hitch a ride

My plan had been to continue down Highway 101, so I wasn't really looking to head towards Nevada, but I generally don't turn down rides when they're offered, so I accepted.

I was going to Nevada.

We packed up all his gear, battened down the truck, and made our way south into California. We cut across to Reno, then made the desolate 200-mile drive down to Pahrump, a small town 20-miles west of Las Vegas.

I spent a few days gambling and sight-seeing in Pahrump, meeting all sorts of folks, even receiving an offer to join a popular local band as their keyboardist. I mulled it over, but San Diego was still calling my name. I went to city hall and grabbed a hold of a map, calculating my next move.

I was now in the desert, so walking didn't seem like a wise option. I didn't really care to hitchhike, either, having just spent 12 hours in a vehicle. I ultimately decided to get a hold of a bicycle, looking forward to riding into the desolate desert of Death Valley.

I spent two days searching for an inexpensive bicycle in Pahrump, hitting dead end after dead end. One of those dead ends was a man I met who was from back east. He and I struck up a conversation about the Mississippi River, both of us having worked on towboats there at one time. He was fired, he told me, for sinking a boat named the "Parham". An odd coincidence, I thought. Unfortunately, the bicycle he had was missing a front tire and had damaged gears.

I finally found a bicycle with two tires at a thrift

store for $5. Unfortunately, it began to fall apart before I even left the parking lot   This wouldn't do for Death Valley.

 Resigned to the fruitless search for a bargain, I took the remainder of my money, literally scraping together pennies, and purchased a bicycle from Walmart. I was now completely penniless, but at least I had thick tires and plenty of gears.

 I strapped on my water containers, climbed on the bike, and set off towards Death Valley with nothing but a few pancakes and the contents of my backpack.

 I spent two days on a desolate desert highway before rolling upon a small group of buildings.

"Death Valley Junction," the sign said.

It looked like a Mexican ghost town from the old west. There was an old opera house, a non-operational cafe, and a small hotel tucked in the corner.

I stepped inside the hotel and was transported into another world. It was like stepping into the 1800s. Hand-painted murals covered the walls, there was piano music playing in the background and a roaring fireplace. Ballerina memorabilia decorated the interior.

The host and maintenance man swiftly appeared, inviting me to sit for a while, to have a cup of coffee and a bit of candy. It was Halloween night, I discovered.

As it turned out, they were renovating the old

Cafe and could use a hand. Having no obligations nor timetable, I volunteered to stay and help in exchange for food, lodging, and admission to the upcoming ballet shows.

As the days went on, this small town showed itself to be wonderful, if not a bit peculiar. The town had a population of five, and all of them worked at the hotel. The hotel would fill up with guests at night, almost exclusively foreigners; poets, musicians, photographers. I even met a Dutch man who was a doppelganger for Gene Wilder's Willy Wonka. He was amused when I showed him the movie, writing the name down for all his friends back home.

For two weeks I stayed, working on the cafe by day, attending the ballets at night. It was a one-woman show, very intimate and exquisite. It had a slightly gothic feel to it. With circus-like music and the aura of the dead-silent, barren desert outside. It was almost as if I were in the Twilight Zone. This town was wonderful.

When they found I could play piano, I was given the opportunity to play as the audience strolled into the shows, playing my own compositions. The dancer even suggested the two of us develop a comedy character for me to play on stage, during the intermissions.

Unfortunately, much to my chagrin, the manager of the hotel had other ideas. Afraid I was intertwining myself into the town, becoming a permanent fixture, she nudged me along. Softly and cordially, but still catching me by surprise.

Feeling a bit bamboozled, I packed up my belongings and climbed back on my bike, setting out for the next town, heading into the heart of Death Valley.

After two more days of riding, I arrived in the small town of Furnace Creek, being greeted by a massive hotel. There were horses and covered wagons parked alongside the roads. Folks in cowboy garb all around, as far as the eye could see. Unbeknownst to me, it was the middle of the annual gathering of the 49ers, when Furnace Creek turns into the old west for a few good days.

I went into the local establishments, inquiring about temporary work opportunities, applying for a position as a bellhop in the hotel. A woman stopped me on the way out, "Matthew!" "I thought that was you!" "Good to see you!".

I had no idea who this woman was, but I hugged her and said hello.

She told me about the festivities going on and said to say hello to her husband, Mike, who was outside by one of the wagons.

Having no idea what Mike looked like, I went on to the local General Store, looking for a friend I had met a couple of towns back. He said he worked here in Furnace Creek and to say hello if I passed through.

I ended up meeting and befriending several of the employees in the town, being invited to a small chili cook-out at their dorms.

These generous people packed my backpack full of food, quelling the necessity to work in the town.

I spent several days enjoying classic country-western concerts, horse shows, fiddle contests. Walking the streets with a group of interesting characters, all loners transplanted from various parts of the country, A blonde-haired, braids-laden girl from Minnesota; a dapper grey-bearded man known simply as John the Hiker; and a soft-spoken young intellect named Zack, sporting a bushy beard and a civil war cap. Drinking Jose Cuervo and whiskey, we searched for the various sources of music and clapping that was echoing throughout the desert streets.

I slept in the desert by night and commandeered a rocking chair outside the General Store by day. I felt at home in this atmosphere and soon had friends everywhere I turned.

One of those friends was a girl from Anaheim, CA.

Hearing of my story and seeing an Anaheim Library Card in my wallet, she asked me if I wanted to hitch a ride with her on her way back home.

Compelled by opportunity and potential adventure, I accepted the offer and headed out with her the next day, leaving my bike behind as a gift for Zack. Unbeknownst to me, Zack had left a surprise gift for me as well, stuffing a shiny new pocket watch into my backpack earlier in the day.

The girl and I hit it off quite well on the way to Southern California. Playing music, talking, sharing stories.

I stayed with her for a few days, enjoying champagne and wonderful food, learning about her and her frequent cycling excursions. Even meeting her family over Thanksgiving dinner. But, soon enough, duty called, and I hopped a bus, riding the final 120 miles to San Diego.

Stepping off the bus, I took a good look around me. Here, on the southern edge of the US, amidst the sights of the city I had set out for 6 months prior.

With a sprawling community of homeless hippies and travelers, the sidewalks near Petco Park would fill up with tents and blankets at night. Bodies lined up on the sidewalks.   I took my place amongst the crowd at night, exploring the cityscape and beach areas by day.

Overall, my time in San Diego was fairly uneventful, save an ambulance ride to the hospital for cardiac problems and a citation for loitering.

   I would soon tire of the city and head back towards the deserts, seeking new challenges and adventures.

Tennessee to New Jersey

(Louisville, West Virginia, Philadelphia)

.

I set off, in the twilight hours of Friday the 13th, leaving the solace of my book-writing haven in Tennessee. With one, loose directive in mind; head towards New York City. A 1,000-mile endeavor by way of foot.

With no idea what awaited me in-between; what adventures might ensue along the way, what people and places might come along my path, I looked at the picturesque Aurora sky, took a deep breath, and stepped off walking down the highway.

It felt good to be walking again, down the country roads. I made my way through Clarksville and Fort Campbell, Russellville and Fort Knox; I slept in wooded areas and fields, under old bridges and next to creeks. Enjoying the spring-time Kentucky weather. I met and shared meals with generous and friendly folks along the way. One lovely young lady pulling over in the middle of town, inviting me along for breakfast. Providing a well-welcomed conversation. A wonderful counterbalance to the long, lonesome walk that preceded it.

Eventually, the country roads began to give way to busier highways and denser residential areas.

I was getting closer and closer to one of the hearts of Kentucky.

Louisville

Out of food and water, I set off into Louisville.

Though I hastily came across supplies. I continued on and roamed the city for a couple of days, observing its eccentricities and night life. Getting a taste of its culture. Fleur-de-Lis symbols, bars, and old architecture. Barbecue joints and music.

When I felt like I had my fill, I began to calculate my next move, looking for a highway to take out of the city. Taking note of the street names and trying to determine my exact location, I went over to a nearby bar and leaned against the wall. As I stood, looking at the map, a fellow from the deck above called down; one of the servers from the bar.

"Where are you headed?", he asked.

I told him my story, about my travels over the years and my current trek towards New York. After a short conversation, he invited me inside, gifting a free meal and a bit of brew. There, I was greeted by a friendly bartender and a pleasant young lady the server had been courting prior to my arrival. After an hour of talking and eating, the server offered to let me crash on his couch.

After a short, turbulent ride with an intoxicated driver, we arrived at a quaint little farm house sitting in a small, sequestered, garden-laden nook; delicately nestled in the urban landscape around it.

Stepping inside, I was greeted by an array of Jimi Hendrix and Beatles artwork. Music memorabilia adorned the walls and shelves, while knitted blankets sat draped on the couches; A warm, cozy environment. A large Siberian Husky and tiny Chihuahua, known as Uli and Boogey were the first to greet me, followed by the server's roommate, Brittany.

She quickly accepted me, herself having traveled for years, experiencing and understanding the lifestyle that comes along with it. Graciously, she invited me to stay for more than just one night

For two weeks, I stayed with the pair, having long conversations, listening to music. Very interesting and genial people. It felt like a small artistic sanctuary.

Sometime during the second week, while reminiscing about past experiences and discussing mortality. we decided to, as a trio, consume LSD and roam the night-time landscape of downtown Louisville; Testing our wits and seeking to create a new adventure. Exploring the bars and diners, meeting various groups of people, holding onto our bearings despite the effects of the LSD.

I fervently recall a stark moment where the server and I, under the peak influence of the LSD, stepped into a tiny bar and were greeted by the blaring music of a rock and roll blues band. Playing on a stage that took up a good portion of the bar, at a volume that could be startling to a sober person. We stepped in and were engulfed by the music. His gaze shot over to me, sweat rolling down the side of his head. With a frantic stare that could only be described as "Dude". A stare which, in that moment, I completely understood and agreed with.

For many days, we enjoyed ourselves, sharing stories and discussing ambitions. I really felt at home amidst the pair. But, as always, adventure began to call my name, and I knew I had to continue down the road. With a heavy heart, I exchanged contact information, said my goodbyes, and set out.

The female, Brittany, would pass away a few months later, being found cold and unresponsive in the house where we had all interacted. An abrupt end to a short life. Her travels and joyful way of interacting with friends and acquaintances did, however, leave a noticeable impact. I certainly value and carry with me the brief time we occupied together. I count it as very enjoyable experience.

Muhammad Ali

Putting Louisville in my rear-view mirror, I began

to settle back into the solace and seclusion of the road. Getting further and further away from the city atmosphere. 5 miles, 10 miles, 15, 20.

 The city blocks turned into neighborhoods, then the neighborhoods into fields. Until, finally, I reached the edge of the county. A giant sign stood in front of me; " You are now leaving Jefferson County". On the edge of the sign, someone had slapped a Louisville sticker.

 Standing there, staring at the sticker, I was overcome by a feeling. A poignant, overwhelming sense that I was not yet supposed to leave Louisville. The forces of nature were urging me back. I sat down next to the sign, shaking my head. Twenty miles out of town, tired, I had very little interest in backtracking. But I knew I had to. Louisville was undeniably calling me back. I didn't know why, but it was.

So, I turned around, trekking the twenty miles back into town, checking into one of the local homeless shelters. There, I sat. I watched. I waited.

Two days later, Muhammad Ali died.

It was an interesting time in Louisville. A historic time. The passing of one of the most popular icons in modern history, born and bred on their streets. Muhammad Ali meant a lot to the people of Louisville.

Sitting in a community drop-in center the morning of his death, I watched the reactions. The images of 60 and 70-year-old black men with tears quietly rolling down their cheeks.

Even if you did not agree with all his views and beliefs, you could not deny the philanthropy that Ali took part in, his work on civil rights and equality; Routinely going out of his way to interact with the community, to spread good will and bring cheer to those around him, one person at a time. For that, I respected him.

The day of his death, walking around Louisville, I felt disappointed by the lack of fanfare. Sure, he had only just passed, but I had expected to see some sort of visible tribute to recognize the loss.

With all eyes on Louisville, I felt there should be some sort of visible commemoration. Resided to this, I scoured the streets and gathered a collection of materials to construct a sign; Scavenging a wooden stake, I constructed and adorned it with a large red cloth-glove and a small rectangular sign under the glove reading *RIP ALI.*

Quietly and somberly, for 10 hours, I carried the sign around every street of downtown Louisville; The city intermittently honking and cheering, raising their fists in the air, taking the opportunity to let go of a little grief and mourn.

As the sun began to lower, I took the sign to the namesake Ali Center downtown and stuck it in the middle of a makeshift shrine of flowers that had begun to form. A fitting place to leave it, I thought.

Over the next several days, the city began to fill with droves of fans and admirers. News cameras, celebrities, and world leaders became a common sight. Small festivities and tributes were held, leading up to the main event; the memorial service that Ali himself had spent years carefully crafting. His final farewell and message to those he would be leaving behind.

The Kindness of a Stranger

Tickets for the memorial service were a very rare commodity. The service was slated to be held in the Yum Center, a small basketball arena laid claim to by the NCAA's Louisville Cardinals. An arena that sported a mere 20,000 seats. Not enough for the local population of 500,000 residents, much less the rest of the world's population interested in attending.

With no ticket, I decided to locate myself around the arena anyway. A distinct feeling urging me to do so. The same feeling I had felt a week earlier that had led me to stop in my tracks and return to the city.

There, I sat, perched on a concrete wall, observing the massive crowds; the news trucks and helicopters; the processions of limousines and police vehicles. Everyone stood, gearing up for the memorial service, Ali's body having already been brought back to the city earlier in the day. It was there, perched in front of the arena, amidst the crowd, that a man walked up to me.

"Excuse me, do you have a ticket to get inside?"
"No sir," I said.
"Would you like a ticket to get inside?"
"Yes sir," I replied.

With that, he handed me a ticket.

Indescribable odds.
But, somehow... I had expected it.

With a ticket in hand, I headed into the arena.

I must say, I was certainly not disappointed by the service. A service planned by Ali himself, with groups of all faiths and viewpoints coming together to share a similar message; *Good Will is the answer, the one thing that will surpass all else. Let all your actions contain it. And for those who are too tired or simply cannot muster good will, at the very least do not show ill will.*

It was a moving service, indeed. One that lifted the spirits of the city.

The Next Step

As the days passed, things slowly started returning to normal. The crowds vacated and the news shifted.

I remained in Louisville for two more weeks,

living amongst the homeless community. Making a point of exploring and taking note of some of the city's grittier aspects. That is, until I came across a flier.

"Travelling Carnival," it said. "Hiring."

 Surely piquing my interest, I gave the number on the flier a call. I set up a meeting with the recruiter, packed my bags, and happily joined.

   In a big red dually truck, we left. Delving into the wooded Kentucky highways and small towns, country music playing on the radio; A sharp contrast to the city life we had just left behind.

After a short trip, we arrived at the Carnival's headquarters; a single, small mechanic garage and an old pole barn filled with carnival rides and equipment. Parked in the grass was a small convoy of campers and pickup trucks, sprinkled with the 15 or so employees of the carnival.

Exactly the atmosphere I was hoping for.

I was quickly introduced to the colorful cast and assigned a room in one of the campers. For the next two days, I settled in. I rested up a bit and helped prepare the convoy for its first journey and stop.

Carnival rides and campers in tow, the line of dually trucks sped off towards small-town Indiana and the community of Lawrenceburg.

For three days, we set up the rides. One by one, like giant transformer toys, we unfolded the trailers, connected auxiliary pieces, and adorned them with lights and decorations. A large amount of work; sometimes heavy, but very satisfying and enjoyable.

With the rides all set up and prepared, we turned our sights to the small town around us. Several of the workers headed off in the trucks towards the local restaurants and bars. My interest, however, turned towards a small side road where there was said to be a large Hollywood-themed casino. An oddity, I thought. An elaborate casino on the outskirts of a small town?

Intrigued, I took off walking, hoofing the three miles of desolate road and eventually stumbling upon a large parking garage, next to which was an entrance to a seemingly large building. The entrance was grand, but I couldn't quite make out the building's exact parameters, the parking garage and trees obscuring my view of the building itself.

Allured by the entrance, I opened the doors and

stepped inside. I was immediately taken aback by the sheer size of the place in front of me. It almost seemed unreal. Illogical. This massive of a building just sitting on the outskirts of a small town?

I walked through dimly-lit giant rooms, movie posters and golden fixtures adorning the walls. Flashing lights emanating from rows and rows of Hollywood-themed machines, filling the void of the giant, seemingly endless cave-like spaces.

But oddly, despite all the lights, all the fanfare and expense, the size of the building, the place seemed... strangely... empty. No one at the machines, no one walking around. I received a distinct feeling of unreality. That I had stepped into the twilight zone. That I was in limbo, temporarily separated from reality.

In that moment, that stupor was broken by the start of a song over the loudspeakers; An obscure song that was uniquely dear and meaningful to me, having played a pivotal role in providing comfort and solace during a recent, defining moment in my travels. Like the sudden appearance of an unexpected friend in a strange place, the sound met my ears.

The twilight-zone feeling intensified.

Like a wave, I was then filled with another, very powerful and familiar feeling. The same guiding feeling that had caused me to turn around and reenter Louisville.

Clearly, without words, the feeling urged me, telling me which way to go, guiding my actions. With no thought, I followed it.

Quite specifically and clearly, it took me to an old-fashioned slot machine. I put $1 in and pulled the handle; I won $10.

"Good, now go to the next one," the feeling urged. As, over the loudspeakers, another pivotal, meaningful song from the timeline of my travels started to play. I followed the feeling to the next machine and put in $1...

A $6 win.

"One more," it urged.

I stood up and went to the third machine. I sat down, put in my dollar and pulled the handle; the lights flashed, and an $8 ticket came out.

I sat there at the machine for a moment and looked around. This didn't seem real. It felt very much like a dream. As if I had been in a coma for the past 20 years, living in a mentally constructed world of travelling, writing, and adventuring; A dreamed-up, imaginary quest of gathering psychological wisdom and helping the world. And that it was now finally crumbling. The illusion was falling apart. I truly expected, at any moment, to wake up in a hospital bed.

As I sat there, contemplating the reality around me, the stories of my travels, the entirety of my experiences over the years, my writings and research, a third song came over the speakers.

The music and lyrics of Natasha Bedingfield's 'Unwritten' began to ring out.

"I am unwritten
Can't read my mind
I'm undefined
I'm just beginning
The pen's in my hand
Ending unplanned

Staring at the blank page before you
Open up the dirty window

Let the sun illuminate the words that you could not find

Reaching for something in the distance
So close you can almost taste it
Release your inhibitions
Feel the rain on your skin
No one else can feel it for you
Only you can let it in

Today is where your book begins
The rest is still unwritten. "

Compelled, I stood up and walked to the center of the room. Unsure of where I was going or what I was doing, I took off walking. Guided by the feeling, turning left, turning right. I navigated the casino until, finally, my eyes hit a machine. Sitting off by itself, in the middle of the floor, with a familiar voice emanating from it.

It was a Gene Wilder's Willy Wonka slot machine.

I stopped. Willy Wonka and its wondrous, fantasy-laden atmosphere was something that I had long identified as sharing and encapsulating the atmosphere felt during my travels. Having been led to this machine, I approached.

Overcome with a sense of happiness and comfort, I sat for a moment, then put money into the slot.

First Pull ---- -$1 prize.

Second Pull --- $1 prize.

A Pause…

I pulled the handle a third time. The machine stopped and went silent. Artfully, an old familiar tune began to flutter out. All else around me went away as I gazed at the machine, still filled with the comfort of the guiding feeling as the words of the song began to play. A strong feeling of a presence all around me.

"Come with me and you'll be
In a world of pure imagination...
We'll begin, with a spin,
Travelling in the world of my creation
What we'll see will defy... explanation.
If you want to view paradise
Simply look around and view it
Anything you want to, do it
Want to change the world?
There's nothing to it. "

   With that, the rest of the casino suddenly came back into my awareness. The guiding feeling and the dreamlike sense faded. But an extreme sense of satisfaction and joy remained. I had heard what I was supposed to hear. Almost as if the Universe had called time out, led me around the casino, and sent me a message. "Keep going, Keep pushing. You are on the right track."

With that, I stepped back, satisfiedly, and headed back to the Carnival. Looking forward to the experience that lay ahead of me.

For over a month, I lived and worked with the Carnival, travelling to and setting up in a total of four towns. In the company of several Juggalos and a young doppelganger for Rob Zombie's Captain Spaulding, I spent most of my time at the top of the giant slide; The highest point in the area, watching over the grounds. Perched in the watchtower on the mountain.

I split from the carnival at the conclusion of our

stay in the small, AIDS-stricken town of Scottsburg, Indiana. Having made a giant circle over the past month, we were now only 30 miles away from the spot where I had joined them, 30 miles from Louisville. The perfect opportunity to pick up where I had left off and resume my trek towards New York. After helping tear down the rides, I said my goodbyes, put on my backpack, and set off.

With a steady pace, I made my way south, swinging through Louisville and intersecting with Highway 60. Barreling east, I cut along the old familiar path, making my way to the Jefferson County sign, the place I had felt compelled to stop at and turn around from two months earlier. This time, however, I was to make it beyond. I placed my hand on the sign, bid my farewell, and continued east.

For 60 miles, I trekked. Not sure what to expect nor what was ahead of me, I strolled on. I passed through several small towns, eventually reaching a steep, windy portion of the highway; surrounded by tall, thick rock-walls, as if nestled in a canyon. Around the turns I went; left and right. Until, finally, I was greeted by the sight of an incredibly tall building in the distance.

Frankfort, Kentucky

The building was an odd sight. It appeared to be nestled directly next to thick woodlands. Almost touching the tree line. Perched on a mountain side, the whole town appeared to follow suit, surrounded by the untamed trees. As if someone had decided to build a large town in the middle of a small pasture in the wilderness.

As I strolled through the heart of downtown,

gazing about, it was quiet. Few faces meandered around, but each one was friendly. It felt like a scene from Mayberry or Leave it to Beaver.

Enthralled, I set up shop and checked into the town's shelter, joining a grand total of four other people residing there. Quite fittingly, it turned out to be the nicest, most welcoming shelter I had ever checked into. It truly felt like being in a warm, southern family-home.

Making friends and absorbing experiences, my time in Frankfort ended up bearing fruits and giving host to unexpected oddities. I met and befriended a young intellect and budding humanitarian, James Fofana. I rather enjoyed hearing his vision for and drive to the build the future. Having come to the United States as a child refugee from the embattled African nation of

Sierra Leone, he ultimately grew up near Washington, D.C. Many fruitful conversations were had, ideas and information being exchanged.

Racial Tension

My time in Frankfort also lead me to bear witness to a very real and poignant example of racial tension, a subject that was very pertinent to the current events at the time, the foggy aftermath of five racially-motivated police deaths in Dallas and the shooting deaths of two black men in Baton Rouge and Minnesota still very fresh.

Here, the tension build was a slow one. It occurred between a homeless former Frankfort police officer who had quit the force several years prior due to disgust with corruption and a black shelter employee who was tasked with supervising the shelter at night and interacting with the residents. I personally watched it escalate over the course of several weeks, fueled in large part by the media reports and the divisive language being used in them.

 The two men were friends when I arrived, taking part in conversations; Mutually enjoying light-hearted television shows and trading jokes. But, bit by bit, as worldly events began to unfold and vitriol began to spill from the airwaves, it began to creep into the shelter conversations.

 Both men were cordial at first, but you could see them slowly becoming more and more defensive and cynical as the days wore on. As they were continuously inundated with the exaggerated language. The contempt for police officers and contempt for the black community echoing over the airwaves, extremist views from both sides seeming to get more attention and favor than the reasonable ones.

Eventually, the men's cordial tones turned to softly spoken defensiveness, then to resentment, ultimately culminating in a physical confrontation where the shelter employee tackled the former police officer, who was left with a broken collar bone. Both men were subsequently barred from the shelter.

Both friends of mine, they came to me afterwards, individually, and shared their stories of what happened. Both men were calm and grounded, and each believed they were the victim in the whole ordeal.

And, truly, they were both right.

Gladly, now a year and a half later, I can report that both men are doing well; having garnered employment, financial stability, and housing.

Kevin Bacon

On a lighter note, my time in Frankfort was also host to an amusingly peculiar and unexpected event. Inexplicably, the actor Kevin Bacon showed up and performed a music concert in the tiny theatre downtown.

I had bewilderedly seen the concert advertised on the marquee of the theatre two weeks prior, but unfortunately, the tickets had already been sold out.

Unwilling to give up on witnessing the concert, I hatched a scheme to ascend into the parking garage next door, leap over onto the roof of the theatre, and attempt to enter the facility through a large air vent on its roof that I had noticed after doing a bit of reconnaissance on Google Earth. Success or failure, either way, I figured it would be a rousing good adventure.

30 minutes before the concert was to start, I walked to the theatre to do one final pass around and observe the surroundings.

Sitting on a bench, watching the passersby, I overhead a lady ask about returning a ticket for a friend that had not shown up. When she was told she could not get a refund, she began to hand the ticket to the teller, uttering, *"Here, then, perhaps you all can resell it or give it away."*

I sprang up.

"Excuse me, ma'am, but if you are giving that ticket away, I could sure use one."

She looked at me.

"OK. Here you go."

Easy enough.

With that, I happily strolled inside.

I enjoyed what was, to me, a peculiar and amusing sight. Kevin Bacon, not 40 feet away, playing guitar and singing in this tiny theatre. Playing and singing quite well, might I add.

Ironically, most of the songs he sang were folk songs about travelling the dusty roads, by foot and

train, with little to no money. Surviving and
drifting.

  As the concert ended, he went off stage and was
out of sight rather quickly. He did, however,
glance my way a couple of times, possibly taking
note of my appearance and my dusty hat. I later
heard rumors that he was spotted in town,
intermingling. In any event, I count it as a good
night.

On to West Virginia

 Bidding farewell to Frankfort, I set off and headed
east. Passing through sprawling farmlands and
race-horse country. Through the towns of Paris,
Judy, and Owingsville. Olive Hill, Graysville, and
Catlettsburg. Finally crossing the bridge into the
state of West Virginia.

At this point, unknowingly, I was only miles away from, as I would later learn, the Heroin-overdose capitol of the United States.

Huntington

My first impression of Huntington was not a pleasant one. Entering from the west, I ventured through one of the city's more run-down areas. It definitely had a gritty urban vibe; A stark contrast to the past three months of small country towns. I felt myself sinking back into city mode; the slightly raised level of adrenaline and awareness that the environment demanded.

Fortunately, the downtown area of Huntington turned out to be quite nice. Though it was, as I found out, rife with Heroin, it was at least kept clean and orderly, and everyone seemed to be polite and respectful.

My first night downtown was spent sitting outside the downtown library. A good centralized location to hold out until morning time.

It was there that I encountered the first of what would be many addicts in the city. As he approached and said hello, I could tell that he had just shot up. Having no plans to leave for the night, I decided to let him use my phone charger and watch over him while he was inevitably incapacitated by the drug.

As morning time approached, a passerby engaged me in conversation and kindly directed me to the city mission, a quaint shelter where I was greeted by a hot meal and a friendly staff. This turned out to be my base of operations for Huntington, a city which ended up occupying nearly two months of my time. Many interesting events and people made appearances during the stay.

LAUNDRY MAN

While at the mission, I ended up volunteering for laundry duty. The industrial sized washer and dryer sat in a back room with a lockable door and a small radio. In exchange for doing the linens, you were essentially provided a place where you could eat, relax, and even nap if you desired. A nice refuge from the rapidly dropping outside temperatures and the increasingly crowded lobby.

 Eventually garnering the moniker of "Mr. Clean", I ended up offering to do folks' personal laundry from 7 pm to 10 pm. Though I didn't charge anything, they were always appreciative and looking out for me, bringing snacks, sodas, and money. An example of good will and respect breeding good will and respect.

COLLEGE DAYS

As it turned out, Huntington was home to the famed Marshall University, its campus lying only a few blocks from the center of downtown.

 True to form, I made a point to experience the University in some way. I explored the grounds and read the plaques, I took a drink from the memorial pool dedicated to the victims of the football team's famed 1972 plane crash. I also sleuthed my way onto the football field and roamed around in the aftermath of a 24-21 homecoming victory, absorbing the atmosphere, participating in the celebration and festivities.

Taking that celebration to the streets, I made a point of visiting each frat and sorority house in the area, briefly going inside, doing a dance, and exiting; Eventually ending the night at a frat house with an old antique fire truck parked in the lawn. Though I generally do not drink, they showered me with alcohol, and I accepted. Handing me beer after beer as I told them stories from my travels. After 13 or 14 beers, I finally called it a night and headed back to the shelter. Unfortunately, the doors were already locked, so I spent the night outside. Crawling underneath a parked semi trailer, I dozed off and heartily rested.

Cubs win the World Series

2016 brought a historic World Series. It featured the Cubs; a team that had not won the series in 108 years, against the Indians; a team that had not won in 79 years. Interesting and enthralling on its own, certainly. But for me, it held special significance.

 Growing up in the 90s, like most of the nation, I was captivated by the historic home-run race between the Cardinals' Mark McGwire and the Cubs' Sammy Sosa. Growing up in West Tennessee, only an hour away from the Cubs' minor league team at the time, I had fond memories of seeing Sosa belt bombs against minor league pitching during exhibition-game gimmicks. I identified with and greatly admired Sosa's seemingly good-natured and compassion-laced personality and gladly sported an old Cubs hat during my years as a youngster.

 Faithfully, I would always tune into the games, undeterred by the perpetual strings of losses.

For them to have finally made it to the World Series, a feat long since deemed impermissible, 108 years since their last victory; It was exciting.

Unfortunately, as it turns out, the city of Huntington lies directly alongside the border of Ohio. And, since West Virginia has no major-league team of its own, the town's residents seemed to overwhelmingly take to the Indians. In the city mission, specifically, I seemed to be the lone individual in favor of the Cubs.

The series itself came down to the wire. In a best of 7-games contest, each team had managed to pull out victories to sit at 3-3. Only one game remained. Winner-take-all.

I convinced the shelter employees to let us

homeless folks huddle into the cafeteria and watch the final game on a big-screen television.

There, I sat. In a room full of Indians fans, I quietly rooted for the improbable, for the Cubs to achieve the seemingly unachievable.

The game went down to the wire. Back and forth, the two teams swapped the lead, ultimately tying in the 9th and sending the game into an extra-innings showdown.

Tension and anticipation riding high, the Cubs finally took the lead in the top of the 10th and sat 3 outs away from victory. We all sat. We watched.

Out number one. *

Out number two. *

 As the next batter approached, the atmosphere was electric. Sitting on the precipice of history, the pitcher squared up and released. The batter slammed the ball into the dirt. The fielder scooped it up, threw it to first base,

...and the Cubs won. After a 108-year drought, the Cubs had finally won.

 The game quickly cut away, giving air to an old Budweiser commercial featuring the legendary Cubs announcer, Harry Caray, a man who died many years ago without ever getting to see the Cubs win it all. But here he was, posthumously, on the television. Looking at the camera, sitting in the old Wrigley Field bleachers, he held up a can of beer. "Cubs fans, this one's for you."

The Road to Morgantown

I exited Huntington during the dead of winter. I had, at that point, garnered the interest of an intelligent and genial young man by the name of Paul who had been struggling with Heroin addiction for the past 10 years. I had begun to counsel him by passing on and teaching him the fruits and lessons of my work and research over the past five years. The mind-mapping process and theory developed from the relentless observing and recording of the brain; its method of triggering distress and joy, how those triggers are determined, the mechanism and derivation of the process of thought, and the brain's storage of memories and the way those memories are prioritized, associated, and recalled.

His enthusiasm for the material led to an interest

in accompanying me on my trek to Morgantown, continuing to study and learn the material on the way. Unfortunately, with the heart of winter setting in, I felt uneasy about bringing someone along with me. I felt it unfair to subject someone to the hardships and dangers that making such a trek posed. Instead, I exchanged contact information with him, hoping to facilitate a reliable means to continue the teaching.

As I had expected, the trek turned out to be a cold one. Full of freezing rain, snow, and biting winds.

With truly inadequate gear, I made do. Timing my movement and improvising ways to stay warm and dry.

Fortunately, generous passersby routinely stopped and offered rides. One fellow I had previously met in Huntington. An older fellow who, due to the financial strain of dealing with terminal cancer, had stayed in the city mission to help make ends meet. Driving on the highway, by chance, he happened to notice and recognize me. He promptly stopped and offered me a ride, ultimately going many miles out of his way to help bring me closer to my destination, eventually dropping me off at a truck-stop in the small town of Flatwoods.

Through strings and strings of small towns, I eventually reached the outskirts of Morgantown. Snow falling and wind howling, I descended down a long, steep highway, making my way into the ridge-laden university town.

On arrival, it was a beautiful sight. Quaint, yet lively. This was to be my home for the next several months. A good place to hold out for the winter.

Settling In

Shortly after arriving, the cold weather having firmly settled in, I decided to check into Morgantown's homeless shelter. Likely the most unusual shelter I had ever checked into. Single men and women, married couples, children; all were mixed into the same facility. One large open room during the day, and a set of 10 small upstairs rooms for the night.

I spent my days both exploring the town - a community built upon and centered around West Virginia University - and interacting with the residents of the shelter.

In particular, I made a point to get to know and befriend the children. Though this shelter was not as rowdy and dangerous as others I had been to, it still presented a tense and stressful lifestyle. For children to be experiencing and braving such a disposition was heart-pulling. I wanted to do my part to bring them a bit of joy. Give them a friendly face amongst the crowd of strangers.

One such endeavor was taking to and mentoring an 11-year-old fellow with a few behavioral problems. Given his current living situation and the fact that, <u>one by one, all</u> the male role models in his life had been stripped from him due to lengthy prison sentences, his behavioral quirks were not unfathomable. There was a big abnormality and void. But I made it my mission to fill that void. To try to give him a shoulder to lean on and an example to follow in an environment where there was otherwise nothing.

It took a great deal of commitment. Day after day, playing games, having conversations. Addressing moments of bad behavior and formulating appropriate and finessed responses. Passing on wisdom and sharing stories. Great strides were made. It did me good to see his progress. He was a good-hearted kid from the get-go, he just needed a little bit of nudging to make sure his behavior and actions didn't go off the rails in response to his situational hardships.

Under Attack

It was Christmas Eve at the shelter. Everyone was winding down, preparing their beds for a good night's sleep. I stepped outside to take out the trash, a chore that I had regularly performed, when a group familiar, friendly faces called me over to drink a beer with them and converse.

We had a few laughs; all seemed to be pleasant and well.

Out of the blue, my buddy turned to me with a serious look on his face. There was an unfamiliar face among the group, and, according to my buddy, the stranger was on the cusp of swinging at me.

"I do not know why", my buddy said, "but he is intent on it." "Would you mind going inside for now so there isn't a fight?"

Bewildered, but unfazed, I agreed. I did not know the fellow and had no issue with him.

As I neared the door, the stranger yelled out. "Punk!" "You're a punk!"

Again, not knowing the fellow and not having an actual issue with him, I was unmoved, but I did feel compelled to retort in some way, for the sake of leaving the situation on a better note.

I turned around and calmly, but firmly, stated: "I do not have a problem with you, buddy. I don't even know you".

That was all it took.

He came charging at me like a bull, ill intentions in his eyes. 30-feet away, I sighed to myself. Here we go.

I remained flat-footed until the last moment, instantly squaring up and delivering a front-kick to his solar plexus.

The wind knocked out of him, I took him to the ground and secured his wrists.

There, as I held him to the ground, I began to notice distinct signs of schizophrenia. With this in mind, I decided this fellow was not likely to be a future threat to me. That this was likely a momentary lapse in his behavior and this was likely to be an isolated incident.

So, instead of striking, I held him there and forced him to calm down.

After a couple of failed attempts to struggle, he finally gave in and listened to me. I addressed his misconceptions and, when I was sure he was calm enough to not try charging me again, I let him up.

This all took place just outside the window of the young 11-year-old fellow I had been mentoring.

As it turned out, the young fellow's father had been put in prison specifically for beating a man to death, less than 1,000 feet away from this particular spot.

I remember walking inside afterwards and hearing his mother tell him "See, Braxton, you can be strong and still use your head." That's when he remarked to me, "You're really strong, Matthew."

As a humorous side note, the moment I took the stranger down and secured his wrists, as I was perched over him, looking him square in the eyes, my arm must have hit my phone in my pocket; because, with inexplicable timing, the mickey-mouse-esque vocal stylings of Tiny Tim's "Living in the Sunlight, Loving in the Moonlight" began to loudly ring out all around us.

I can not describe to you the momentary look of confusion and fear that came over his face.

The road to Philadelphia

With spring rearing its head, I decided to leave Morgantown behind and continue my journey. 300 miles from Philadelphia, I headed north, crossing into the state of Pennsylvania and continuing on for 40 miles before turning due east onto the historic Lincoln Highway. Passing through a mixture of old steel towns and vast countrysides, I stumbled upon Amish farmlands and even inadvertently encountered 9/11's Flight 93 crash site and memorial.

Rescue in Uniontown

Though my time in Uniontown was fairly brief and uneventful, my departure is worth a mention. For my exit of Uniontown, I boarded a city bus for a brief 10-mile ride down the highway, enjoying a break from the usual ground and pound nature of my travels. Stepping off the bus, I continued on foot for several minutes before realizing I was missing something;   my phone charger.

I must have left it on the bus.

  With no money to replace the charger, I headed back towards the bus stop, waiting the hour or so it would take for the bus to come back around.

  After a bit of patience, the bus finally returned. I boarded and looked for the charger; no luck. Empty-handed, I exited the bus and it drove away. It was then that I spotted something odd.

  At the edge of the bus stop sat a large, extremely-steep gravel hill that led down to a set of railroad tracks. On the side of this hill, halfway down, there was a 70-year-old man, a bottle of beer in hand, slowly sliding down the hill. The tracks were directly at the bottom of the hill; if you slide down the hill, you will land on them. These tracks were active, too; I had personally witnessed two trains go by in the previous hour.

Moving quickly, I yelled down to the man. He was very disoriented and uncoordinated. I tossed my backpack aside and descended down the hill, reaching the man and grasping his hand. Systematically, I pulled his weight and kept my footing, slowly pulling him up the hill. When we reached the top, I carried him to a nearby tree and propped him up, sitting and conversing with him for several hours as he slowly began to regain his sobriety. At the end of our conversation, with the subject of the phone charger having not been mentioned, unprompted and unexpectedly, he handed me the money I needed to replace the charger.

An unusual string of events, I felt. Almost as if the charger had been taken from me so I would return to the bus stop and assist the man, then, reparationally have my phone charger replaced.

Lancaster and Strasburg

The city of Lancaster was surprisingly normal. Though neighboring Mennonite churches were prominent, there was very little noticeable Amish presence in the town.

After exploring the town for several days, attending Mennonite services and interacting with residents, I set out to find the actual Amish communities. Eventually, I found what I was looking for, venturing into the small neighboring town of Strasburg. Filled with buggies and a sprawling Amish population, the town had a cheerful and friendly atmosphere, even amongst the non-Amish folk mixed within.

Late one night, sitting outside the town's library, two teenagers on their bicycles stopped and engaged me in conversation.

"Excuse me, mister. Are you travelling through?"

"Yes, I am on foot, headed towards New York City, but I decided to stop here for the night and take refuge," I said, pointing to a large front of approaching storm clouds.

"Well, there's a church nearby that leaves their doors unlocked. They have internet, snacks, and sodas. They wouldn't mind you taking shelter there for the night."

How peculiar, I thought. You do not see that very often. While plenty of churches are welcoming, I had not encountered one that indefinitely leaves

its doors unlocked. Nor have I heard of a town safe
enough for it to do so.

Happily, I followed them to the church, telling
stories and answering their questions about my
travels.

Eventually, we reached a small Baptist church.
Just as they said, the side door was unlocked.
They led me inside to a small room. The lights
were already on. A big sign adorned one of the
walls "Welcome to the Well. Make yourself at
home."

After taking down the name of my website, the
young fellows wished me a good night and exited
the building. After a bit of meandering, exploring
the dark, moon-lit halls and sanctuary of the

church, I enjoyed a soda and bedded down in the illuminated community room.

Sometime in the night, I awoke. Needing to urinate, I stood up and made my way towards the restrooms on the other side of the building. As I exited the dark hallway and stepped into the open floorspace, the silence was broken by an ear-shattering alarm and series of lights.

Quickly and calmly, I went back to the room, gathered my gear, and exited the building, setting off down the dark highway away from town.

Though it might have been a mistake, though I might have truly been perfectly welcome in the church that night, I couldn't be sure. Being a stranger in the town and not knowing the names of the fellows who had suggested the sanctuary, I did not feel it wise to be at the scene when the police arrived. I spent that night on the outskirts, lying low in the cover of darkness.

At daybreak, I made my way back towards the library, intending to acquire a map and calculate my route east.

Arriving a bit early, I sat on a bench outside the library doors, waiting for it to open. As I sat there, I began to notice parents bringing children into the closed library. Every few minutes, a new parent and child would appear, giving me a suspicious look as they walked in the door. After the fourth child, it occurred to me; they must have a daycare service here.

Realizing I am an odd-looking fellow, a stranger to this small, intimate town, carrying my backpack and gear; I promptly stood up and relocated myself to a bench farther away from the building.

Not unexpectedly, a police cruiser pulled up a few minutes later. The officer, happily, was very polite and courteous. He thanked me for preemptively moving away from the door, assuring me there was no problem. He warmly welcomed me to the town and explained that his approach was nothing more than mandatory contact in response to a call.

After a short, pleasant conversation, he reentered his car and drove away.

Ten minutes later, he returned.

"You weren't at a church last night, by chance, were you?"

Hmmm.

Taking the honest approach, I told him the story of the storm and the offer of shelter I had received. Noting that the cameras would support my story of no wrong-doing.

Satisfied with my story, he thanked me and drove away.

An hour or so later, while using the internet, I received a friend request and message on facebook from the pastor of the church. He apologized for the alarm and assured me I was welcome at the church.

Good.

After thoroughly examining the map and calculating my route, I gathered up my things and continued down the road.

Nearly There

For another week, I barreled, making my way towards the city of Philadelphia. As I edged closer and closer, residences and businesses once again became more frequent and the highways became busier. Only 20 miles out, and night time setting in, I decided to go ahead and bed down.

I eventually spotted a well-illuminated church sitting in a cove on the hillside. Despite my recent experience, I decided to give this one a chance, albeit outside instead of inside. Figuring it to be a safe, neutral place to sleep, I ventured up and laid out a blanket on the side of the building. As I prepared to bed down, a car pulled into the parking lot. The driver exited the vehicle and began to approach.

I stood up and rolled up my blanket. "Hello. Forgive me if I am trespassing," I said, "I am headed to Philadelphia and was looking for a place to bed down for the night."

The fellow approached and, with a warm, smiling face, greeted me. "That's not a problem," he said. "Are you hungry?" "Do you need anything?"

He took out his keys and unlocked the church doors.

Walking inside, he handed me a giant case of

granola bars from one of the closets.

"This should last you until you get to Philadelphia."

Graciously, the man offered to purchase a hotel room for me for the night, even offering to stop along the way and acquire a meal from Burger King. Continuing the rush of good will, he contacted me the next day, asking if I would be willing to accept a train ticket for the remaining 20 miles to the city. Appreciative of the generosity, I accepted.

Philadelphia

After being dropped off at the station, I prepared to board the train to Philadelphia.

Paring down my gear, I threw away everything but the bare essentials. With no money, no place to stay, and no work lined up, I was going to be starting on the streets. For this reason, I wanted to be as mobile and flexible as possible. The less gear, the better. I also wanted to be sleek and blend in (as well as someone with my appearance could.)

Not the Philadelphia I Expected

Everything I had ever seen of Philadelphia had led me to expect a tough, blue-collar town. A collection of construction and factory workers, laboring all day and decompressing in the pubs at night.

Instead, I found a very artsy city. With an air of

elegance. Friendly, too. Street musicians on every corner. An exceptionally diverse collection of businesses and entertainment venues.

 Certain areas of the city, I would find, did have quite a bit of danger and grit, but even they didn't carry the old-time Philadelphia reputation. These areas had shoot-em-up urban gang-violence as opposed to the old-town individualistic grit.

 Still, I was determined and intent on making the most of what the city had to offer; Experiencing its culture and eccentricities, whatever they may be.

 Stepping off the train at the 30th street station, I set off and spent my first five days exploring the layout of the town. Exploring for 20 hours at a time, I would catch a nap in a sequestered nook or alleyway, then head back out to continue traversing the crowds and taking in the sights.

Looking to explore more of the city's underbelly and street culture, I ultimately decided to check into the downtown homeless shelter.

As I stepped in, I didn't quite know what to expect. I was no stranger to shelters, nor to large cities, but Philadelphia had a reputation of being tight-knit and wary of outsiders. If this reputation were going to rear its head anywhere, I figured, it might very well be here.

With that in mind, I prepared myself and entered the door.

What I wasn't quite prepared for, however, was

to be, as far as I could tell, the only white fellow there. Making me even more of an outsider.

 Now, truly, race was not something that mattered to me. I had been the minority many times in my travels, in many different situations. But, I had never been the minority figure in a Philadelphia shelter. With Philadelphia's reputation, I had to wonder; would this environment be receptive or suspicious and hostile?

 I couldn't be sure.

 But, if there was one thing my travels had taught me, it was that despite our differences, deep down, people are people. Respect, integrity, and good will are Universal languages.   Show them, and those around you will eventually appreciate them, and you.

With that notion, I plunged in. Sitting back at first, I watched. Silent and poised, like a sniper, I waited for small opportunities to offer brief interjections in conversations. A poignant comment, a short story, a joke. Anything to create a pleasant moment and interaction. Slowly, bit by bit, gaining traction and favor; interaction by interaction, individual by individual.

Before long, I had intertwined myself into several small circles. Making acquaintances, being invited to tables, and ultimately making friends, leading to more opportunities to step into more circles and eventually cover the entirety of the shelter population.

I took great joy and interest in these interactions. Gleaning information and listening to stories. Getting insight into many unique perspectives.

The shelter environment was, however, fickle at times. I took great care to orchestrate my actions and closely manage the environment and people around me. Always aware. Walking a thin line, combining the right amount of forcefulness and strength with an equal amount of good will and compassion. A combination that allowed me to make friends and allies without being mistaken for possessing weakness and vulnerability.

I spent several weeks in the shelter, observing my new peers in their day to day activities. Roaming the city with them each day. Occasionally going off alone to find and participate in one of the endless number of odd or special events taking place in the city. Stumbling upon marathons, street performances, rallies and demonstrations.

An Unexpected Turn

Eventually, I began to seek out work, looking to see what the city's business and commercial side had to offer. Going to the different staffing agencies downtown as well as following individual leads from construction sites and workers.

It was at this time that I came upon a rumor of an odd work opportunity. Once a year, they said, at about this time, a white van shows up in the heart of downtown Philadelphia and picks up a group of workers. They shuttle them to the middle of nowhere, to a remote workcamp in the farmlands of North Carolina. Sorting and loading potatoes in a pole barn. It is rough, they said. There are fights, there are drugs and prostitutes, there is alcohol. But, if you keep to yourself, watch your money, and keep your wits about you, you can come away with a sizeable sum.

Intrigued, I sought more intel, eventually obtaining the rumored location, date, and time of the van's arrival. So I went. In the center of the city, at 6 in the morning. I watched. I waited.

Bit by bit, a small group of workers began to gather and congregate, backpacks and luggage in hand.

At the turn of 7, right on schedule, a large white van appeared and pulled to the sidewalk, hazard lights flashing. The group hustled to the window, each grabbing a place in line, wistfully waiting to speak to the driver and secure a spot in the van. When my turn came, I received an odd look. A look of surprise and hesitation. Undeterred, I introduced and presented myself.

After a few moments of deliberation, the driver motioned for a few of the workers to climb in the van.

She told me and the remaining workers to show up the next day, that she might return and take one or two more with her.

Eager, hopeful, and undeterred, I showed back up the next day and waited. Right on time, the van showed up. The driver gave

me and the other few workers a once over and motioned for us to climb in.

I would later find out that the hesitation was due to the fact that, besides me, the entire farm was staffed by African Americans. That, were I hired, I was to be the only white fellow there.

Luckily, on the previous day, unbeknownst to me, one of the workers in the van had vouched for me, having previously met and interacted with me at one of the homeless luncheons downtown and found my demeanor to be pleasant.

Good will goes a long way.

North Carolina

Upon arrival, the word remote was proven to be a very accurate description.

After a 400-mile van ride, we had arrived on a vast stretch of sprawling farmlands. With nothing but the treelines and horizon in sight, we pulled up to two small metal buildings, each outfitted with 8 lock-and-key dormitory rooms.

I hastily grabbed a room, bunking with a fellow I had befriended in the shelter back in Philadelphia.

Our first two weeks on the camp were spent leisurely. With the work not yet starting, we were free to enjoy the quiet freedom of the farm. The summertime days and nights.

Though we had not yet made any money, we were given the opportunity to purchase alcohol and food on credit, leading to small barbecues and get-togethers.

I took this time to get to know my new compadres; Mostly city folks from the streets of Philadelphia and St. Louis. Some had been here before, but for some, this was their first exposure to the wide-open country.

I rather enjoyed observing them in their new environment, seeing how they adjusted and what effect it had on their day-to-day activities and habits. Watching their reactions to our frequent critter visitors; Snakes, opossums, mice, coyotes.

Though I was the only white fellow, I was readily accepted and fit in well with the group.

Day after day, week after week, we walked to the pole barn and sorted potatoes. The trucks and combines would harvest in the fields all around us and bring us truckload after truckload.

After a long day, everyone would shower and enjoy their free time. Some went to their room and rested up, some stayed up all night and partook in the drugs and alcohol that had made its way onto the premises.

  Though there would occasionally be a fight, folks were mostly cordial and considerate. Being in the country, away from the tension and aggression of the city environment, folks were able to tone down their cold demeanor and open up a bit. Settle in and allow room for more friendliness.

  Monday through Sunday, we labored. Getting shuttled to town on Saturday nights to pick up food and supplies to last us until the next week's trip. For those who spent all their money on drugs and women, they resorted to eating spare potatoes and bony fish from a nearby pond.

  As the summer wore on, the temperatures rose and the work days became longer. Some left, catching buses back to the cities from which they came. But for those of us that remained, we grew closer and developed a comradery.

As May turned to June, then June to July, the potato supply began to whittle down and the seasonal operation drew to a close.

We each said our goodbyes, received our final paychecks, and began to prepare to return to the places from which we came.

Those of us who had come from Philadelphia piled into the old white van and prepared ourselves for reentry into the hustle and bustle of the cityscape.

Philadelphia, A Different Side

My return to the city was a stark one. The van pulled in and dropped us off in the same place it had picked us up two months earlier. The city was just as we had left it. We, however, were now different. Many experiences richer, many friends richer, and $1200 richer. We all shook hands, wishing each other luck, then parted ways, venturing back to our previous lifestyles, disappearing into the city's endless waves of people.

I spent my first few days walking around, seeking out and rendezvousing with a few old faces. Learning about some of the events that had taken place while I was gone. Learning that someone had been stabbed to death in the shelter shortly after I had left.

Having already tasted the homeless lifestyle, I decided, this time, to experience a different side of the city. On a whim, I checked into a hostel in the heart of downtown; a cheap community boarding-house filled with mostly international backpackers and travelers. With 20 beds to a room and large open community spaces, it was the perfect place to meet and study various types of people; Often playing games and interacting with large groups, many different nationalities being represented.

Russian, Argentinian, Swedish, Spanish, Irish, Turkish, Australian, Ukrainian, Syrian, German... Many fantastic and enlightening conversations were had.

At one point, I came across and met a pretty, young red-headed gal from Britain. While demonstrating my arguably odd method of dancing, I turned around and first laid eyes on her, staring at me with a sincerely dumbfounded look.

Fortunately, she seemed to think well of the dancing. I introduced myself and we proceeded to get along quite well. I was intrigued.

A Moment, A Heart

One day, I overheard her plans to visit the nearby Revolutionary War museum. Knowing she was a history fiend, I deemed this a good opportunity to create a memorable moment and outing.

Trailing behind her, I stealthily entered the museum and went ahead of her. I climbed my way to the top of the stairs, suavely posting against a wall in preparation of her passing by. As she appeared at the summit of the steps, her eyes caught sight of me. She gladly approached and hugged.

We proceeded to tour through the museum, making tongue-in-cheek jokes and musings about our perspective differences in heritage and culture. Amusedly noting how vicious the museum was in portraying the British.

Ultimately, the visit culminated in a small, dark auditorium centered around the subject of George Washington, the historical figure that she had expressed the most interest in.

There, on a stage, not 20-feet away, behind a closed curtain, waiting to be revealed, sat the actual tent that Washington had carried and slept in every night of the war.

Sitting next to the girl, complete darkness around, the stage illuminated and the curtains began to rise. I looked over at her and clasped her hand, looking her in the eyes, then shooting a gaze back at the stage.

250 years after a bloody war between Britain and the US, sitting only paces away from the battered tent of the architect General, sat an American and a Brit, in solidarity and unity, hands clasped and hearts together. A wonderful moment.

Having our own plans and itineraries, we subsequently spent only a brief amount of time together before having to continue on our respective paths. But, it stands as a well-crafted and happily recalled set of moments.

One Last Hurrah

My remaining time at the hostel was relatively brief. After my interactions with the girl, I spent an additional week in the facility. I befriended several people, using my recently acquired funds to visit and enjoy the city's eats and scenery.

One such outing was an amusing trip to the pub with a fellow from the British country of Wales, Mr. Simon Davies. A bicyclist, he was in the midst of a 2,000-mile journey from New York to Los Angeles. Still in the beginning of his journey, he took to me, seeking stories and advice on travelling the US.

We sat and talked, enjoying beers and occasionally listening to the pub around us. It was a lively one, too. The patrons routinely singing along to songs on the jukebox.

Fittingly for my new friend, the Beatles' "Hey Jude" came on. Happily, we put our conversation on hold and joined in with the diverse group of jolly pub patrons.

To keep the event going, I went over and put on Queen and David Bowie's "Under Pressure". A rousing success; The entire pub joined in and gleefully sang along.

My British friend then went over and put on one of his favorite songs, Oasis' "Don't look back in Anger". Unfortunately, it fell flat. My friend began to happily sing, but the rest of the pub sat silent, staring at the jukebox.

Poor fellow.

He soldiered on, however, and continued to sing along. Happening to like the song myself, I raised my glass and joined him.

On to New Jersey
 The day of my departure, as a farewell send-off, I went and had a large pint of apple cider with Mr. Davies. I wished him well on his journey, then strapped on my backpack and headed off towards New Jersey.

 Crossing the Ben Franklin Bridge, I entered the crime-ridden Jersey town of Camden.

 Not too long ago listed as the most dangerous town in America, Camden has a reputation for routinely yielding one of the highest rates of murder per capita in the US. In 2012, it had a higher rate than Detroit and Chicago combined.

Though it had eased up a bit since then, it was still a stark contrast to the clean and artsy landscape of downtown Philadelphia that sat just across the bridge.

I had crossed the bridge into Camden once before, briefly, during my initial stay on the streets of Philadelphia. Not knowing the history of Camden at the time, I was taken aback by its crumbling infrastructure and run-down nature. Quickly picking up on its vibe and atmosphere, I began to tread more carefully.

My first human encounter was only in passing; A gentleman coming towards me on the sidewalk.

As he neared, he held out his hand, giving me a container full of some sort of pills. "God Bless You," he said. I thanked him and continued on.

Uninterested in the pills, I disposed of them in a trash can. I did, however, out of curiosity, take note of the brand name on the container. Now, it's possible that the container was just a placeholder; that its original contents had been discarded and replaced with a new type of pill. But the container itself, according to Google, was a brand of heavy duty laxatives.

In any event, here I now was, back in Camden. With New York City less than 100 miles away, my direction was laser-focused. I roamed around Camden a bit, taking a look at more of the infrastructure and grabbing a bite to eat at a chicken shop. With money strapped to my calf, I went to the local bus station and hopped a bus to Trenton.

There, I ran into a recent acquaintance from Philadelphia. A fellow who had once selflessly shared food and tea with me. As it turned out, he too was headed to New York City.
Unfortunately, having met him in Philadelphia, I knew he had very little money to purchase a train or bus ticket. Without him asking, I purchased a ticket, putting him on the next train and wishing him well.

Myself, however; I had to walk. At least partially. I needed to adequately experience more of New Jersey.

Though it was pouring rain, I set off onto Highway 1 out of Trenton.

Navigating treacherous stretches not suitable for foot traffic, I continued down the dark road. Climbing over guard rails, carefully balancing on the concrete barriers of overpasses.

For 28 miles, I continued, passing through the towns of Lawrenceville and Princeton. At this point, my shoes had failed me. The bottoms were coming loose and the insoles had fallen apart. The resulting contortion and pressure points led, several miles later, to quite a bit of discomfort and pain. Intermittently stopping and removing my shoes for relief, I continued my trek north.

Eventually, I reached the small high-rise town of New Brunswick. Looking at the map, I made the decision to hop train to Newark. I climbed the large hill to the town's train station and took the stairs to its tall, open-air platform. It was quiet and chilly. To your right, you could see the neon lights of the high-rise buildings. To your left, nothing but the dark night sky. Tired and sore, I laid down and rested.

I awoke to the sound of a screeching transit train. This was the one I was after. I boarded and took my seat.

After a brief 5-minute ride, we arrived at the Newark station. I hopped off. The accents around me sounded familiar. The way folks were bustling around; I was getting close to New York.

After exploring the town and conversing with some of the old-time locals, I set off towards my final destination.

Following the shoulder of the Newark Jersey City turnpike, I crossed over the water into Jersey City. Planes flying overhead. Helicopters visible in the distance.

I trekked the final few miles through vehicle-only tunnels and overpasses, climbing walls and hopping barriers. Down into Hoboken, to the edge of the Jersey Island, all the way to the banks of the Hudson River.

Standing there, staring across the river, the night-time lights of the Manhattan skyline in perfect view; The sight that I had envisioned over a year and a half earlier, that had driven me over 1,000 miles through six states.

One thought echoed through my mind.

"I'm coming for you."   "Soon."

"Not yet."

"But soon."

Bonus Stories

Here are a few non-sequential excerpts. A small set of quips that did not make it into the larger stories, but that are still worth sharing.

To Keep the Bears Away

In Oregon, while in the mountains with Dave, the gold prospector.

While hiking and dredging the creeks for gold one evening, I stopped and began to inspect one of the hillside rock-slides. Unfortunately, not realizing I had stopped, Dave went on ahead of me, disappearing out of sight before I noticed.

We were already many miles up the creek, away from the campsite. We were in a very remote area, and the hillside that led to the campsite was not very distinguishable or marked. Dave knew what it looked like from his months of using it, but I certainly did not. With this in mind, I figured I would stay put and wait; If he went on ahead, up the creek, he would surely have to come back down to head towards camp.

Unfortunately, the minutes turned to hours, and the hours stretched on. As the sun began to set, I knew something was off. Either Dave was stuck up creek or he had slipped by me without me noticing. Either way, I was going to be bedding down in this spot for the night. The creek itself was filled with giant boulders, fallen redwoods, and massive rock slides. It was like the ultimate obstacle course. Certainly not something to try to traverse at night, to reach an unmarked destination that you can not recognize.

To make an unfortunate situation hairier, this section of the creek sat in a large canyon, surrounded by unstable ground and recent rockslides. Sleeping at the bottom was a risky endeavor, but climbing it or heading down creek was not an option, either. Bears and mountain lions were also common in this area.

As the cool wind and darkness of night began to settle in, I looked around for pieces of material I could use to build a small shelter. Aside from rocks, however, there was very little. One or two pieces of wood sat lodged in the side of the hill, but I decided to leave them be, less I weaken the hillside and cause another avalanche of rock.

I ultimately acquired three small slabs of wood from the water and positioned them against the side of a boulder. It wasn't much. It was probably the most pitiful thing I had ever built. But it was enough to stick my shoulders, head, and neck into.

The wildlife in the area was not particularly used to humans; we were in a pretty remote area of the mountains. Though I had a 40-caliber pistol on me, it wouldn't do a whole lot of good against a curious bear that might accidentally stumble upon me while investigating my scent. I needed some way to ward curious critters away.

That's when I recalled my phone in my pocket. Though it didn't have service, it did have music on it. With the pistol in one hand, I turned the volume on the phone all the way up and selected a song. As I laid my head into the tiny shelter, I listened to Neil Diamond's "Sweet Caroline" echoing throughout the canyon. Happily and soundly, I drifted off to sleep.

The next day, I decided to take matters into my own hands and head down the creek. I knew that eventually, within 20 miles, the creek would empty into the river which would then empty in the ocean in town. A sure way to get back to civilization.

Fortunately, about two miles down the creek, I ran into Dave and his dog, Mister. He had returned to the camp the previous day and set out the next morning to try to reconnect with me. He was worried that something had happened to me, as I was worried something had happened to them. Fortunately, nothing had happened to anyone, and several of the wilderness critters were treated to an overnight concert of Neil Diamond music.

The Grand Quest for Snacks

In Tucson, AZ. Late one night, I had acquired a few dollars by way of bartering. Hankering for a few snacks and soda, I decided to trek a few miles across town to reach a 24-hour grocery store. I arrived, purchased several bags of goods, and turned my sights back towards my rail-side home, a small bed I had made under the concealment of a small cactus tree near a set of railroad-tracks.

Having good knowledge of star navigation and direction, I decided to take a more direct route. Head directly west instead of following the curvy, overly-long main road.

Unfortunately, halfway through, I began to encounter obstacles. Chain link fences, dead-end roads, tall walls. This journey had become an ordeal... n a part of town I didn't recognize. However, I stuck with my star navigation, of which I was confident, and determinedly continued west.

Eventually, I ended up on the interstate. Far away from anything recognizable and unwilling to turn around, I stared at the fence-laden concrete barrier lining the western side of the freeway.

Inside the fence appeared to be a large, active trainyard. I jetted across the interstate and carefully tossed the groceries over the fence, then climbed it myself. Once on the other side, I was taken aback by what was in front of me. Directly in my path sat 15 tracks, all with trains on them. Trains that stretched as far as the eye could see, left and right. No way to walk around them. My only option was to hop over their hitches, where the traincars were connected to each other.

Unfortunately, I wasn't alone in the yard. Two security SUVS were patrolling inbetween the trains. Going back and forth, with giant spotlights, inspecting the yard and the traincars.

Tired, but still determined, I picked the perfect time and tossed my groceries over the first train's hitch. I then climbed over it myself, picked up my groceries, and hid. Once the SUV passed by, I tossed the groceries over the next train, then climbed over. Like a real-world game of frogger, I hopped each train, tossing and climbing, until I finally made it over the final track.

At this point, I knew I had to be close to my sleeping camp, but I was exhausted. Brazenly, I made my way over to a debris pile in the yard, set out my blanket, and laid down to rest. Listening to a radio show and enjoying the soda before drifting off to sleep.

I awoke the next morning to the sound of bulldozers and large trucks traversing the yard. In the daylight, I would be visible. I needed to leave the yard.

Unfortunately, sometime during the night, a group of fire ants had made their way to my blanket and backpack. Though they had not bitten me, they were all over and inside my gear. I carefully emptied my pack and shook the ants out, trying to stay concealed and quiet while doing so.

Once the ants were out, I geared up and walked out of the yard. Heading west, I soon began to recognize my surroundings. Within a half a mile, I reached my destination. Finally back to the rail-side cactus tree. Though most of the snacks were now gone, having been eaten on the journey, I was still happy with the trip.

Proximity to Tragedies

An odd coincidence, I found myself in the area of two consecutive nation-captivating mass-shooting events in two different states.

While in the town of Gold Beach, I sat one day at the library computers. Drinking a small carton of milk, I pulled up the national news, as I usually did, and noticed something a bit odd and familiar. The national headline read "Mass Shooting at Umpqua Community College"

I sat for a moment, then looked at my milk. It was Umpqua brand milk. I then heard a fellow at one of the other computers begin to cry.

Apparently, Umpqua community college sat in the small town of Roseburg, Oregon, only 130 miles away. Many of the people in Gold Beach had friends and family who attended the community college. Roseburg was a frequent stop for residents of the area, sitting on a popular commute route. The tragedy hit home for Gold Beach, and It had a decided effect on the area.

Exactly two months later, I was in Joshua Tree, California, a small town on the outskirts of San Bernardino County.

Not 70 miles away, while I roamed the roads of Joshua Tree, a mass shooting took place in the county seat, the city of San Bernardino. Deemed an act of terrorism, 14 people were killed in the attack. Sitting only a few miles from a Marine Corps base, Joshua Tree had a strong military presence. With this shooting being done in the name of terrorism, it added insult to injury for this small California town.

While the proximity to these events was purely coincidental and holds no real significant value, I still found it to be an odd occurrence. One that I preferred not continue to repeat itself.

Movie Wedding in Oregon

Gold Beach held a lot of significance in my travels. Taking up three months of my time, a lot occurred there.

One such event took place late one night while I was hunkered down next to the grass banks of the river. I awoke to an odd sound. A faint, distant sound of music and vocals floating in and out with the wisps of the wind. Curious, I listened for a bit, then stood up and followed the direction of the sound.

Through the woods, I reached a windy road. The sound was louder, but still, there was nothing around.

I trekked up the road a bit, then I saw it. On a giant hillside, sitting in the distance, was a ritzy property. Sitting at the very top of the ridgeline, lights and sounds emanating from the building.

I made my way down the road towards the hill. It was quite large. Probably 130-feet high. Rocky and steep. Down below, there was a private road. Gated and guarded. Every few minutes, a fancy sportscar would pull to the gate, then head up the long windy private road to reach the top of the hill.

What was going on up there? For two months, I had seen nothing of this sort in Gold Beach.

I had to investigate.

Looking at the gate, it was too well monitored, and the road sat inbetween rocky hillsides.

Hmm...

I walked around and inspected the hill. It was steep. Climbing in would be treacherous. But... it could be done. But should I?

I should.

I tightened my belt, secured my bootstraps, and stealthily jumped onto the hill.   Carefully and quietly, in the cover of darkness, I made my way up. Disappearing into the trees, grasping at the steep hills of dirt and rock. Careful to not slip and go rolling down.

Bit by bit, I edged my way up, eventually reaching the top.

There it was. Sitting on the other side of a large open field, there was a large barn-like structure. An extravagance of lights and sounds coming from it.

As I would later discover, this was the wedding party for Cody Walker, the brother of the deceased Fast and Furious actor, Paul Walker. Having helped fill in for his brother in one of the recent movies, the event was filled with movie crew and personnel.

Tired from the climb, I sat for a moment, looking out over the horizon. Sitting above the treetops, I had a clear view in all directions. As I sat, staring at the starry night, Journey's "Don't Stop Believing" began to ring out from the building, engulfing me and echoing out into the open, distant horizon.

I sat for a bit, then began to stealthily make my way across the open field. In the distance, I could see a tower-like structure with a silhouette walking around the balcony. Cautiously, I sat still, listening to the deejay, music, and speeches coming from across the way. I timed my movements, scurrying a bit closer each time the figure turned to walk in the opposite direction.

By the time I had made it halfway across, I surmised that the party was coming to a close. People were slowly beginning to trickle out. Being covered in dirt and clearly having the look of a destitute traveler, I knew I would not blend in if spotted. And, as more folks exited the building, the risk of being spotted was getting increasingly larger.

As the deejay bid everyone farewell, I turned around and carefully edged my way back across the field, reaching the hillside and climbing my way back down to the road.

As I walked back down the road, passing alongside the guarded gate, I made eye contact with one of the attendants. He looked at me with a suspicious gaze.

I couldn't help but sense that he knew.

.

Vol II

There are more stories to be told. Stories from the past as well as the stories that are currently taking place.

However, opportunities to adequately write and compile material into presentation form are exceedingly rare, so these manuscript updates often get an expedited send off. I intend to compile and release much more material in the future. More Volumes will be coming.

There is, however, still more to this book.

The following entries are taken from a notebook that I started seven years ago, prior to my travels, just after returning from basic training for the National Guard. I have kept it with me through all these years, continuously adding to it as I went.

Unintentionally, it ended up being a written record of my mind. Simple, matter-of-fact observations. A record of my mind's preferences, desires, reactions. Its emotions, their triggers. A huge collection of facts. Not only to clearly define what gives the mind pleasure, but to also identify and address its turmoils.

(Turmoils = Dissatisfaction, Distress, Frustration, Restlessness, Fear, Anger, Grief; Any unpleasant feelings.)

The idea being that if you take all the turmoils, deconstruct and abolish them one by one, you will

be left with absolutely no turmoil at all. No
problems, at all. You will be completely free of
burden and worry, leaving you with solace. True
and complete peace of mind.

  Though it might sound hokey and unrealistic, I
can wholeheartedly speak to its authenticity,
having gone through the wringer of the process
and come out on the other side. Your turmoil is
not only abolished, but you gain a complete
understanding of the mind. You gain a roadmap. A
clearly-defined operator's manual that tells you
what the mind seeks and why it seeks it. How and
why it reacts the way it does. What makes it
happy and what distresses it. Allowing you to

make it perpetually happy and keeping it from ever being distressed.

It puts you in a state of serenity and contentment from which you never come down.

It is simple to do, too. It does not require a lot of thinking, nor a whole lot of effort. Just time and clear direction

Just get a pen and a notebook. Any time you feel joy or dismay; sadness, anger, heartache; write down the feeling and what event or thing caused it. Do not get hung up trying to explain WHY this is the case, just record the facts of what the feeling was and what the event/thing was that caused it.

Anytime you desire or long for something, write down what it is. Keep it short, simple, and matter-of-fact.

Your goal here is to get a notebook full of these things, these facts.

You will find that as you get more and more of these tidbits in the notebook, things will begin to group together and patterns will emerge. Things will start to become clear, on their own, without you having to do much thinking or analyzing.

Pictures and explanations begin to paint themselves, on all subjects. Small at first, then larger and larger as time goes on.

The notebook becomes an irrefutable rock to hold on to, a reference to look to and a guide. All the answers you seek begin to materialize in the notebook.

If you ever have a question or need help, you can visit www.DrifterJournal.com to contact me.

THE OBSERVATIONS:

Though your notebook will be slightly unique, for mild amusement, I will share some general conclusions and observations that have come about as a result of my experiences and the notebook I have kept.

These are not the instances where problems and turmoil have been worked out, they are just general anecdotes derived from my experiences, observations, and travels.

02/2016

I do not speak on Karma as a mystical force, but...

I do prescribe to the idea that your actions can affect those around you, which in turn affects you.

If you cultivate an environment of bad will, make others angry or put them in a bad mood, it can negatively affect you. You are now around people who are angry and full of negativity, and their interactions with you are filled with such.

If you cultivate an environment of good will, make others happy and put them in a good mood, it can positively affect you.

You reap the rewards. You get to exist in an environment of good will and positivity, and others' interactions with you are filled with such.

On a similar note, if you leave things open to happen in the future, they will eventually happen.

I believe in setting yourself up for success by quelling/dismissing any potential causes of future strife.

If you see that someone has a penchant for getting angry and arguing, odds are that will occur in the future. Either fix that individual, remove them from your surroundings, or find some way to ensure that you will not be subjected to it. Otherwise, given time, it will happen.

If you see that a dog has a history of attacking humans, and there is nothing to suggest that this tendency has changed, you should either cure the dog, remove the dog from your surroundings, or find some way to ensure that you will not be susceptible to being attacked. Otherwise, given time, you are likely to have it happen to you.

 Set yourself up for success. Address the hazards now so you will not be affected by/subjected to them in the future. It keeps your future bright, clear, and optimistic.

06/2015

It is a wise idea to stay Humble. To not delude yourself or have an improperly inflated sense of your role, status, skills, or achievements.

It keeps your awareness of yourself, the things around you, and your place/relation to those things accurate and informed, helping you function effectively and move forward/navigate in a proper and effective way.

If you do not keep yourself humble, something will eventually come along and do it for you. Give you a reality check and put you back in your place, showing you the truth. Save yourself that trouble and all the missteps to which a lack of humility leads.

04/2014

Often, you can't control the outcome of a situation. You can only control the action that you take at the time. It is then left up to other variables not in your control.

If you take the action you feel is right, the one you feel good about, you will have the satisfaction, good feelings, and contentment of that to hold onto, regardless of the outcome.

If you take an action you felt wasn't right just to try to get a good outcome, and that outcome doesn't materialize, what do you have to feel good about?

Liked action with a bad outcome = At least you took an action you felt good about. At least you have that satisfaction/comfort.

Unliked action with a bad outcome = Absolutely nothing redeeming/satisfying about the whole ordeal. Nothing to hold onto.

06/2013

Expectation can have a very large effect on how you feel/react to something.

Did you expect the movie to be great, but it was only good? You might be disappointed/disgruntled.

Did you expect the movie to be awful, but it was good? You might be pleased/satisfied.

Same movie, different expectations, different feelings/reactions.

For a practical example/application of this, imagine having a job where you do not have a set end time. Sometimes you end at 5 pm, sometimes you end at 10 pm.

If you go into the day expecting to get off at 5 pm, you stand a good chance of being disappointed and having to work later than you expected. A 6 pm end-time, even, will be disappointing.

If you go in expecting to work until 10 pm, you are guaranteed to not be disappointed. If you work until 10pm, it will be what you expected. If you get off any sooner than that, you will be pleasantly surprised. 5 pm, 6 pm, 7 pm, 8 pm, 9 pm, 10 pm.

None of it will be disappointing.

02/2015

For those who miss something.

...a place or a way of life. The past.

What are the things you liked about it? The things you miss? What did you have there? What did you do? What did you feel?

Can you recreate it somewhere else? At least some semblance of it, something similar to it? Piece together those same qualities/components?

Really think about it. Really give it some thought. I think the answer is very likely yes.

02/2016

What is Love, for me?...

A draw to someone who provides an overwhelming amount of stimulation to you. An urge to be around that person and that pleasurable stimulation they provide, those intoxicating feelings. They are essentially a drug.

You become protective of that person, sure. You value them. You are fond of them. They are giving you massive amounts of stimulation, making you feel good. They are a wonderful thing to you. The thought of that being taken away can be dismaying.

They are an assortment of different dopamine-releasing things, stimulants. What are some of those specific acts, those specific things that cause Stimulation?

-Physical touch

-The aesthetics of their face, their body.

-Pleasurable smells

-Sexual Intercourse

-Mental Stimulation, Conversation, Sounds

Is it possible to be drawn to more than one person at once? Sure. There are plenty of people on the Earth capable of giving you these things.

Heartache/Heartbreak, in my experience, is the overwhelming desire for this stimulation combined with the disappointment and frustration of not getting it. You see it there, in front of you, you imagine what it is like to partake in it. It is ripe for the taking, but you aren't getting it/can't get it. The desire, disappointment, and frustration hits all at once. It is a very powerful concoction.

10/2014

-When it comes to problem solving; mechanical, mental, or physical,

I like to shun others' explanations and commonly accepted solutions.

Instead, I approach it from scratch, looking at all the elements and circumstances and using my own logic and experiences to come up with a solution. I've found it gives you a much better understanding of the problem/subject, and a better understanding of the solution. It is also a good way to boost/train your ingenuity and problem-solving skills.

You become very effective at accomplishing goals because you can effectively craft, tinker, and adjust solutions and methods. You become more effective at overcoming obstacles. A modern-day MacGyver.

02/2016

Anger, yelling, passive aggressive acts and snide remarks. They introduce bad feelings to the person dishing it out and to everyone else around. Even if it isn't directed towards them.

It is my experience that shows of anger, animosity, and ill feelings are a waste of time and do not assist you or add to any situation. They tend to complicate and muddle arguments. They become a sideshow and distraction. The anger, yelling, and posturing become the focus of the situation instead of the actual points and facts, instead of the actual issue at hand. They muddle everything while also introducing bad feelings to you and everyone around you. Anything you think you are accomplishing by using them can be accomplished much more effectively without them.

You can be stern and imposing without yelling. You can act decisively, directly, forcefully, and effectively without getting angry. You can express displeasure and disappointment without being passive aggressive and snide. You can make ultimatums and draw lines in the sand without being hysterical or ugly. You can be strong, stoic, and forceful without being ill.

Even when met with someone else who is yelling or becoming hysterical, you can remain stoic and calm. Standing your ground, not entertaining or processing the illness. Using logic to assess the issue and dictate your words and actions, tackling the problem head on. Avoiding the dance of posturing and putting on a show.

Let me tell you, once you identify ill-feelings as being unnecessary and cutting them out, a big weight is lifted off your shoulders, knowing that you will never be subjected to the rollercoaster of emotion and distress that they bring. You will never be subjected to that turmoil and dismay.

And for those around you, those closest to you, for them to know that they will never be subjected to that rollercoaster in your presence, that they will never have to be exposed to yelling, tension, animosity, or ill feelings by you, is absolutely invaluable. You are a pillar. A trusted ray of light and source of stability.

11/2017 Perspective

Before addressing or reacting to someone else's actions, there is great value in understanding their vantage point and the reason they took the act they did.

It not only ensures that your reaction is appropriate and fitting, but it can also help you see how to more effectively stop or prevent their harmful acts. Allowing you to formulate the best-targeted and most effective solution.

Ask yourself:

What did they do?

What were they trying to accomplish?

Did they think they were being reasonable and fair? Was it a good or bad intention?

For me, the most important thing is someone's heart behind their actions. Whether they think they are acting in a reasonable way for the sake of good or whether they are acting with malice and unjust intentions.

For example:

One of your friends, while walking with you, starts speaking bluntly and starts making sharp comments towards you. Their voice is raised and their tone is forceful. "You're walking too close to me." "You're killing me with your pace. Slow it down."

It appears they are being intentionally sharp and rude, almost confrontational.

Then, through questioning, you find out that they are having a schizophrenic episode, causing them to have high energy levels. Being bombarded with thousands of thoughts, racing through their mind at once, and a great difficulty in keeping their speech stifled or putting finesse and tact onto their words. And, because of the high energy levels, the speech is coming out louder and more forceful.

That actually, they are not trying to be rude towards you. That, in fact, they are doing everything they can to hold it in, going through great lengths to try to keep it as calm as possible when around you. Their intentions are not ill. No disrespect wanted or intended.

Since the intention is pure and the acts are not harmful, it is not a problem. Though, had you not examined their situation and intentions, you might have taken it the wrong way.

Truly Harmful Acts with Good Intentions

Sometimes, however, someone will have good intentions behind an act, but the act itself leads to harm. In this case, you recognize that their intentions are good and applaud them for it, but you recognize and take measures to stop their harmful acts.

For example: A child watched a string of horror movies where aliens landed in people's ears, slowly infecting the ear, then spreading to the brain, taking over the brain. The kid remembers this movie and it stays with him.

He overhears one day that his friend has an ear infection. So he panics, remembering the movie. He wants to help his friend, so he takes a knife and cuts his friend's ear off.

In his mind, he's doing a good thing. Saving his friend from what he erroneously thinks is going to happen. So you cannot fault his intentions. However, the act was still harmful, so you need to take measures to ensure it will not occur again; address and fix it. In this case, you would educate the kid about ear infections, explain to him that movie was not real, showing him who made it and how. Explaining to him the consequences of someone losing an ear.

Intentional Harm with Ill Intentions

Someone who is knowingly, intentionally causing unjust harm, whose intentions are not good; Their action has to be addressed and stopped, and their psychological disposition of wanting to do ill-willed harm must also be addressed, as it is something that can cause them to do harmful acts again in the future. In this case, the knowledge of what they did, what they were trying to accomplish, and why they desired that outcome is exceptionally useful. If you know the underlying motivation and desire behind their ill-willed actions, you can help them find a way to quell or satisfy that desire in a non-harmful way. Figure out a better way to get what it is they were seeking to get.

10/2016 Knowledge

No matter how much knowledge you have amassed. No matter how wise or knowledgeable you are on a subject, there is always something more you can learn about it.

Even if you think you have reached the highest understanding of a subject possible and cannot fathom anything more, new experiences and bits of information can always come along to take your understanding to a higher level, or fill in gaps that you were not aware were even there.

Do not rest on your laurels because you think you have reached the top. Keep seeking and staying open to additional knowledge and information. I have had this proven to me over and over again.

On a related note, when having discussions and debating topics with folks, it is a good idea to do a quick self-check of your motivation and intentions. If your goal is to intellectually progress or gain knowledge on a subject, then you should avoid the trap of the ego. Avoid trying to prove yourself right. Avoid defensiveness, digging into your positions and closing yourself off to others' input and suggestions. Do not prematurely dismiss their challenges.

If they are telling you that your conclusions are mistaken, at least consider what information or experiences they have that are leading them to think that. Who knows, they might know something you do not. They might show you a new perspective that you have not seen.

 Consider your own experiences and knowledge PLUS theirs.   You might find that your conclusion *was* in fact mistaken. Or, you might draw a new conclusion that neither of you saw coming.

 The purpose is to gather all the knowledge you can. For you to end up with accurate information and an accurate understanding.

To truly, at the end of the day, <u>be</u> right and knowledgeable.

Not defensively close yourself off to maintain the *appearance* of being right and knowledgeable.

08/2013 DREAMS

In my experience, dreams take your recent thoughts, feelings, and experiences and puts them together to create a story. Everything in your dream is related to a thought, experience, or feeling you had recently. You can usually trace it back.

Watch a military documentary? You might dream that you are in a war zone. See a striking car commercial? You might be driving that car around the war zone. Hear coyotes howling while you were outside? There might be coyotes chasing your car around the war zone. Think about a pretty girl during the day? She might be with you in the car.

Dreams seem real while you are having them. The experience seems genuine. You see, hear, and interact with things just as you do in the real world.

For that reason, they can teach you a lot about decision making. You can observe/assess decisions you made during various situations in your dream. Particularly during high-stress, split-second situations.

They can put you in unusual or extreme situations, exposing you to previously unencountered circumstances, provoking thoughts, ideas, or realizations that had not yet been provoked in the real world.

02/2016

On writing and recording:

I can make elaborate explanations, construct a theory, one that ties up all nicely and sounds good.

But if it's not true, it's worthless.

I take great care in what I write and the conclusions that I draw. Being careful to not assume, speculate, nor make unwarranted leaps. I only write what is observed to be true, based on rock-solid facts and experience.

My advice to anyone writing or drawing
conclusions is: Take a step back. Look at what you
are writing. Is it true, or are you making
unwarranted leaps, unwarranted connections,
assumptions, statements? Are you forcing it? Is it
convoluted?

Remember; No matter how nicely you sum
something up nor how neatly you tie it together, if
it is not true, it is worthless and unrewarding.

Keep this in mind if you start a notebook. Keep
everything true and matter-of-fact.

The feeling of absolute peace and the desire for that state.

The Peace of Mind that you eventually gain from the notebook is absolutely wonderful. Indescribably so. Complete contentment and solace.

If you stick with the notebook and reach that Peace of Mind, my advice to you at that point is to take a look at your environment. Cut any requirements or obligations. Anything that tries to restrict you.

Then, as always, for good measure, indulge in some form of Stimulation. Music, food, sex. Whatever you happen to enjoy.

Peace of Mind & Untied Environment + Stimulation = An indescribable, Euphoric Bliss. That never ends. Truly a paradise. I am immersed in it, even now, and I can tell you that it is invaluable. I highly recommend it.

Before I could really put my finger on it and pinpoint it, I spent years grasping at that feeling, dancing with it, trying to put it into the right words, to really understand what I was desiring and how to get it. I would grab a hold of it and describe what I was seeing, painting vivid descriptions of that feeling.

For mild amusement, here are some of the entries over the years where I tried to grasp a hold of it. I'll post the original entries as well as the retrospective assessments of those entries.

The assessments use the terms:

Peace of Mind = All turmoil understood and quelled. Absolutely no problems, worries, or dismay. Completely unburdened.

Untied Environment = Unrestricted, Unbothered, Unobligated. Whimsical Surroundings and Circumstances

Stimulation = Any source of dopamine or serotonin release.

06/2014

-Experienced this while in hotel room-

Room encased in concrete, in the middle of a never-ending blackness. Nothing else in existence but this room.

All alone. Like a blissful purgatory. Timeless.

All is exactly as it should be. Perfect.

Fantastic. Wonderful. Ultimate relaxation and satiation. Ultimate satisfaction.

(Absolutely Untied Environment, Neverending. Absolutely unbothered.)

02/2015

Fantasy. Separated.

Cold, open, beautiful desert. Sunset, sunrise, rock formations in distance. Hills. Only vegetation is sparse brush and cactus. Wide open.

As if I am an Indian, Geronimo, teleporting from one spot to the next, at my whim.

No people. No future. No past. No worries. No needs. No need for food. Just there. Exist.

Teleport from one spot to the next. One rock cliff to the next.

Like being on Mars. Clear night sky.

Reminds me of those mornings in Willcox, sun rising, in the desert. Going to see Keira. I like. Feels right.

(Written as an envisionment of and desire for Absolute Peace. An Untied Environment. Unending. Envisioned here in the form of separation, quiet, and solitude.)

06/2014

Late at night

Lights on, but nobody around

All is fake

Like being in a miniature

Enjoyable

Feels right

Feels like... my place.

(Untied Environment. Quiet. Alone.)

10/2014

In night sky, Darkness all around. Stars.

Euphoric. Restful. Peace.

Non-changing. Beyond time.

Guided by feel. Hedonistic. Bliss. At my whim.

Eternally, forever there. Sentient Being.

(Untied Environment. Never-ending)

11/2014

Arabian Desert at Night

Moonlight shining, gives a bluish-white tint to the sky, the desert, everything in it.

Torches in ground, burning

Separated. Otherworldly.

I, the Shaman, guide my followers. We live.

The environment is... as if... it is the world in its original state, before organisms arrived.

A barren, lifeless landscape.

Barren, Sandy, Rocky, No life.

(Absolutely Untied Environment, with a community of folks that provide Stimulation.)

12/2014

The world is my bed. Sit and lie down wherever.

Nowhere I have to go or be. Doesn't really matter where I am.

No requirements. No restrictions. Time doesn't really matter.

No preparations. No worries.

Meander.

No people.

Food everywhere.

An empty world. At my whim. Comfortable. Roam around. No unenjoyables. Twilight Zone. Blissful.

(Absolutely Untied Environment. No problems, worries, restrictions. Whimsical. Unbothered.)

02/2015

No real purpose.

Teleport, one spot, the next.

No food, water, or sleep needed.

Mindless. Whimsical.

No future, past, interactions.

Cold Bite; open, barren desert

Rock formations, Hills, Canyons

Clear, Dark, Stars in Sky

Otherwise flat land

Just the world. Just... there.

I watch. I see.

I don't think. I just am.

(Absolute Peace. Untied Environment.)

11/2017

Ice Cavern; Antarctic landscape. Barren, lifeless.
Encounter a small cave-like opening in the ice.

Soft white and pink light emanating through the
opening and its walls.

Cold, clear, starry sky. The slow-rolling wind chilling
all as it passes through.

Climb into the cavern, into its depths. Unknowing of
what lies below, what lies beneath. The possibility of
getting stuck or trapped, getting pinned in a narrow
place; no one around to know or help.

But it allures. Its aura of shelter and warmth. Its lights and glow. Its wonder and awe. Possibility and unknown. A portal to another world? A sanctuary and safe-haven? A whole new ecosystem and landscape deep down? What lies below/within?

My hope? I hope to traverse a labyrinth of tunnels, further and further, into the depths of the ice and earth until stumbling upon an open pocket; a dark open cavernous room, miles below the surface. The path of twists and turns to reach it unfathomable and unmappable. Surrounded by the thick, impenetrable layers of earth, rock, and ice. All alone there. A safe-haven of quiet and solace. Warm and secure. Writing, drawing, thinking, resting.

(Untied Environment. Quiet. Solace. Stimulation.)

10/2017

 Daytime. Walking in a major city. But it seems sparse. Almost no one around. The main, large buildings sitting quietly in the midst of the surrounding blue skies.

 Stumble upon an old high-rise apartment building. Inside, halfway up the building, I find a single 3-story apartment. It looks dated. Old, dark-wood interior. Things are still in place from the previous residents. Bits of unopened food in the cabinet. Ancient appliances and furniture, from the 1920s or 30s. Everything immaculately in place, aside from dust covering it all.

It looks as if it had been abandoned and forgotten. Untouched for 90 years. A portal into the past. A step into a forgotten time. All its resources and amenities, but completely abandoned. Quiet and barren.

(Similar to the visions of being the last man on Earth. No other life in existence. But all the resources, structures, and items remain. As if all life had disappeared in a rapture-like event. I explore the Earth, the structures. pilfer through the resources and survive. It is quiet. It is peaceful.)

(Untied Environment. Quiet. Solace. Plus the stimulation of exploring and using the resources.)

01/2015

-Texas

-Dusty Dirt Road

-Dirty Windshield/Truck. Sun shining in.

-Sage Grass

-Sun Shining Through

-Spread out. Mostly farm land. Low Census.

(Untied Environment. No people nearby, Quiet.
Also imagining the Stimulation of the warmth of
sitting in the sunlight and the bright, vivid visuals
of the fields, roads, sky, and trees.)

02/2015

Freedom

No worries.

Roam.

No required future.

On salt flats, dusk, neutral temperature.

Walking, just walking.

Sit, sleep, sit up, watch. Get up, walk, climb. Sit down. Lie down. Sleep.

(Absolutely Untied Environment Unbothered. Mindless. Roam. Whimsical. No problems, no worries. No concerns or requirements. Blissfully unburdened. An Absolute Peace.)

I found Peace of Mind, of course, through the notebook.

For an Untied Environment, I generally hit a small desert town where I have a small piece of land. I can sit on my land, in the sun, and not be bothered. Going in to town, meandering around, all at my whim. No restrictions, worries, or obligations.

Another version of that Untied Environment has been found by being on the road. Going from place to place. Untied, unbothered, unrestricted. At my whim, free. Nowhere I have to be, nothing I have to do. No hindrances.

Being on the road, drifting through the cracks in society. Detached from it, floating. My constant movement allowing me to interact with it without ever being part of it. Keeping me separated. Keeping me in a world of solace. Keeping me untied.

While floating and moving, for my amusement and stimulation, I treat the world as my own personal canvas to create stories, to create adventures. Using myself as the pen and the world as my paper. I sit and think, with the whole world at my disposal, what I could do next. What story/path I would like to create.

I also find that the larger and larger the backstory becomes, the more and more adventures and experiences pile up, human interactions become increasingly more interesting and pleasing. Seeing folks' faces light up with excitement and intrigue when they hear of the path I have been on, the stories and adventures I have endured, my observations and findings on life and the mind. The slew of invitations to events and excursions from those wishing to be a part of or further the story in some way.

It is all welcomed and enjoyed,

So, I continue on this yellow brick road. Having already reached mental paradise, I stroll along, basking in it, nudging those I meet towards it, too.

Though the second iteration of the book is at a close, we will surely speak again.

Until next time, take care, my friends.

Vol II

Vol II

Come on bootstraps, let's go.

Journey on down this road

I know it seems cold and so far from home

But I promise it leads us to sunshine and gold.

Come on, bootstraps, let's go.

On to the seas, we'll go where we please.

Travel through hardship and pain and disease.

Learn when we triumph and grow when we bleed.

All for the knowledge and wisdom we need

To learn how to be happy and peaceful and free

Come on, bootstraps, let's go.

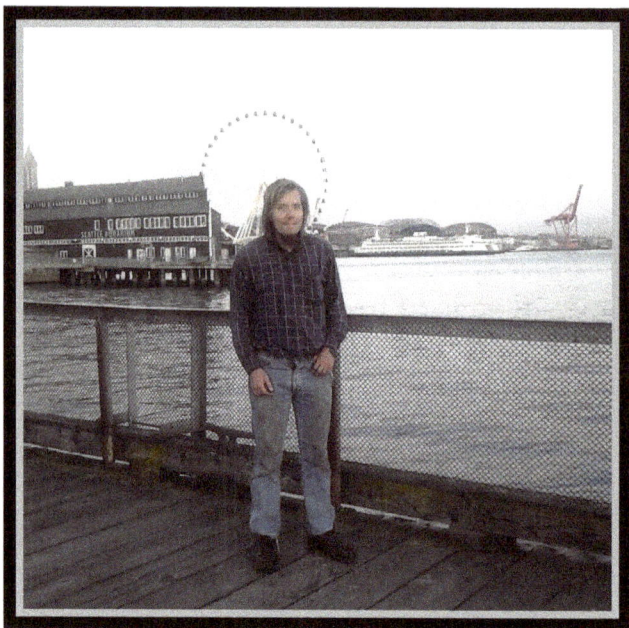

In Seattle, preparing to head out on foot towards Oregon.

The end of a long day, on the heels of a multi-town trek,
resting outside the library in the beach town of Port Orford.

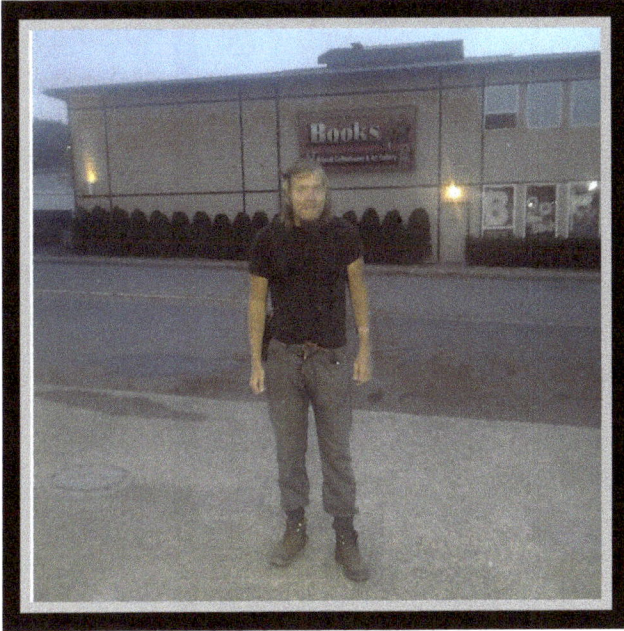

In Gold Beach, Oregon, nearly to California.

In Pahrump, Nevada, looking towards Death Valley

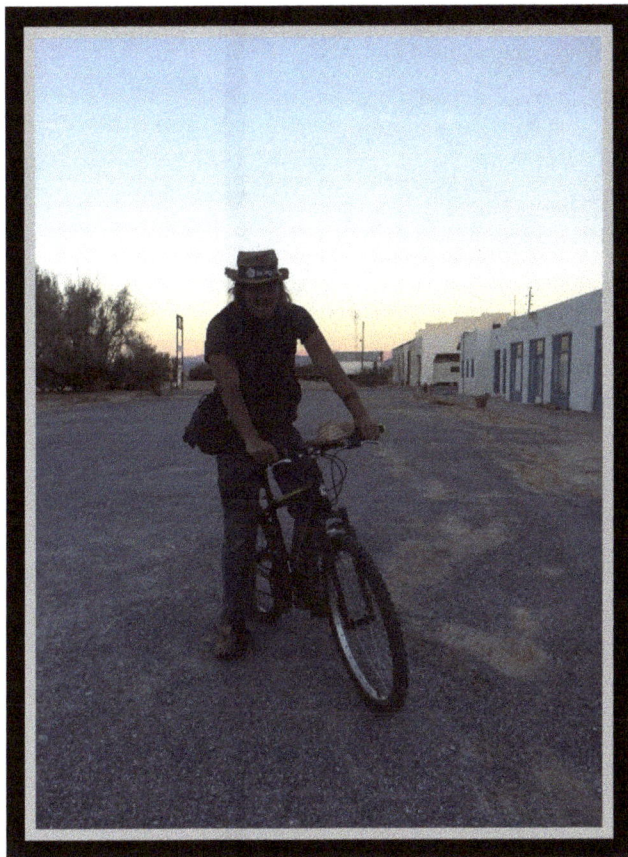

In Death Valley Junction, headed towards Furnace Creek.

Arrival in San Diego

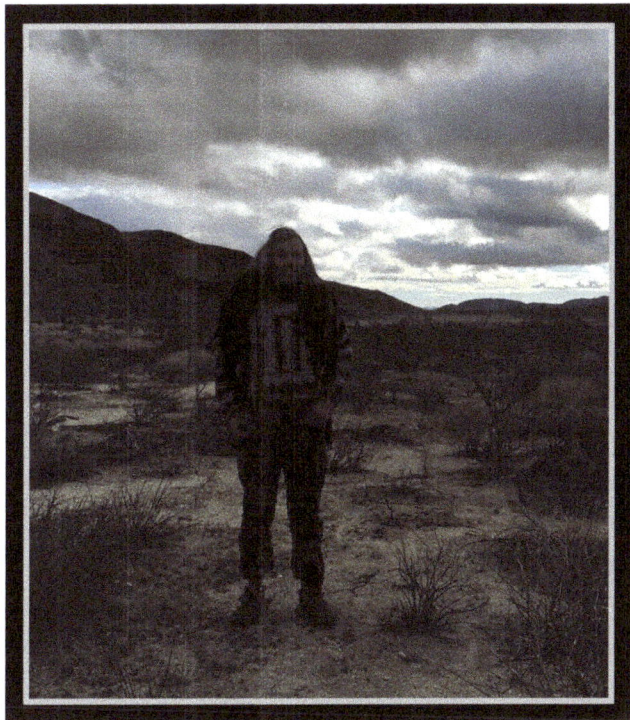

The beginning of a 50-mile trek through
the canyons and backroads near Joshua Tree, CA.

On the outskirts of Louisville, KY, preparing
to head into the city to gather food and supplies.

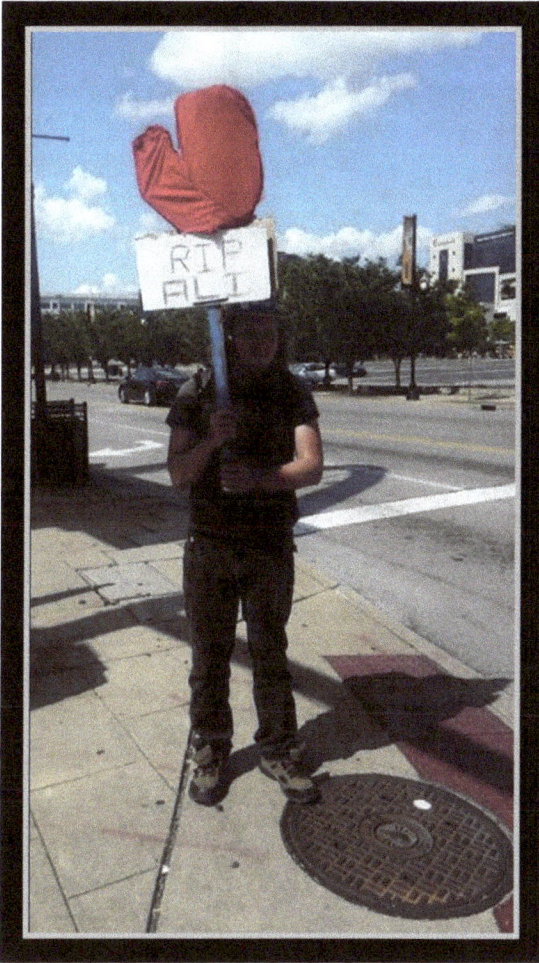

Amidst the Muhammad Ali funeral services in Louisville, KY.

Working with a travelling carnival out of Kentucky.

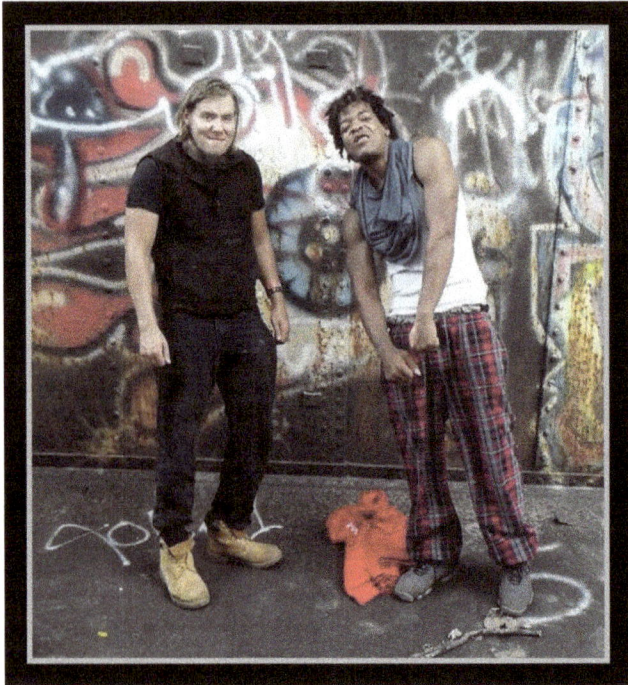

Amidst friends in the small city of Frankfort, KY.

Kevin Bacon in concert; Frankfort, KY.

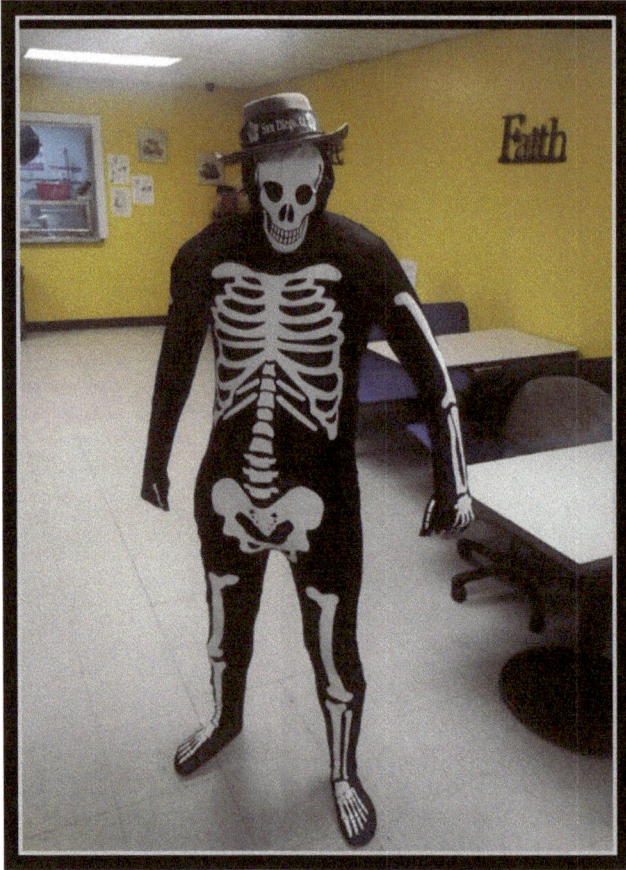

Frankfort

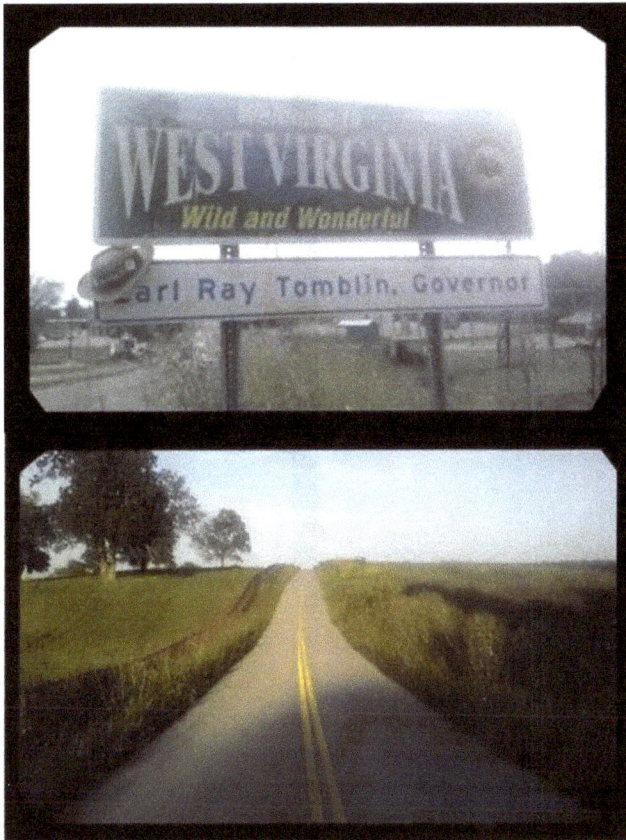

Down the highways and through the hills
of Eastern Kentucky, into the state of West Virginia.

In the back alleys of the city of Huntington, WV.

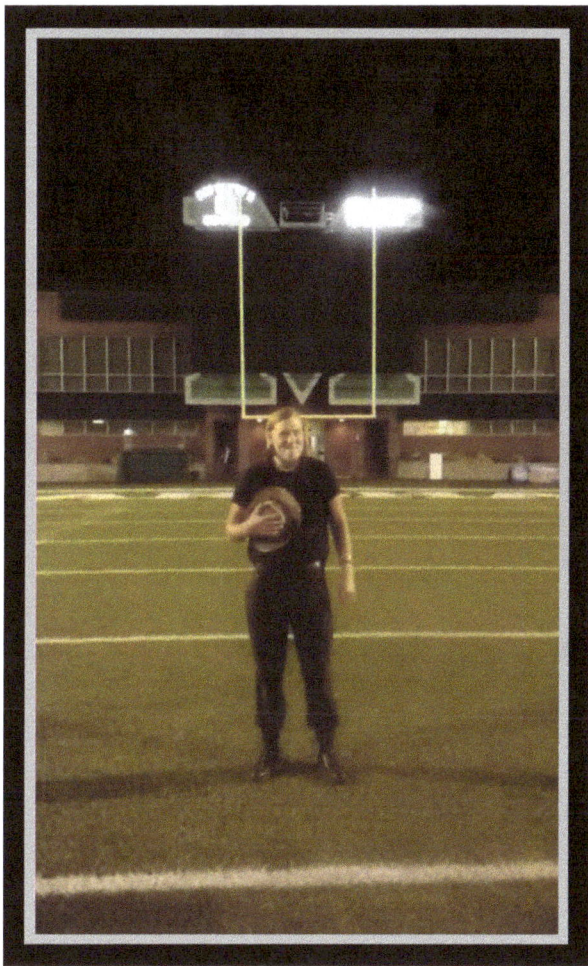

On the field of Marshall University, following a 27-21 home win.

My friends from the shelter in Morgantown, WV.

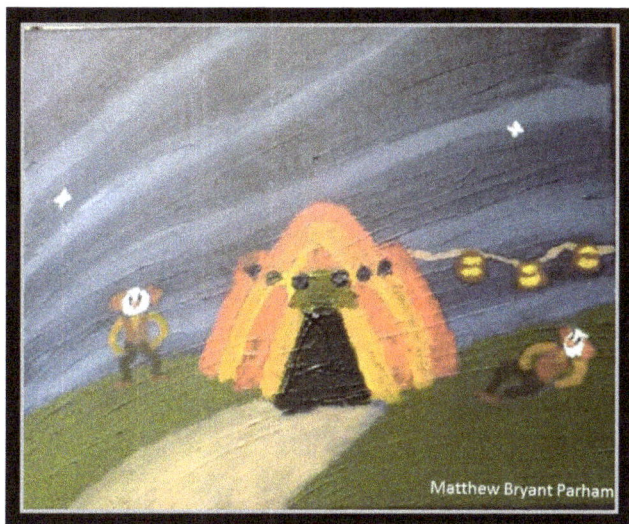

My masterpiece painting: *Clowns in Space*

Originally hanging in the Friendship House in Morgantown.

Preparing to trek into and across the state of Pennsylvania.

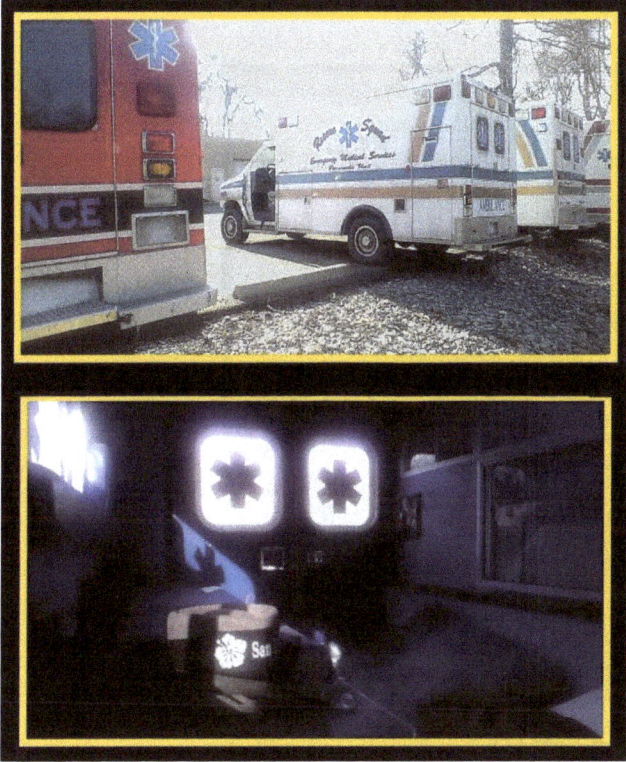

Finding places to sleep on the highway; Opportunism

Philadelphia 2017

North Carolina Potato Farm

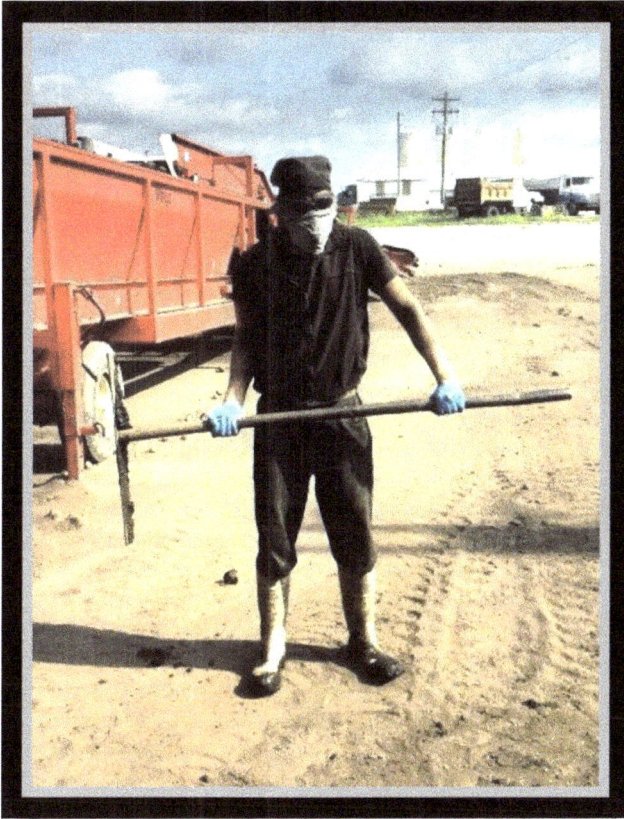

Amidst the hot, dusty summer days on the farm.

On the banks of the Hudson River in Hoboken, NJ.

Staring out across the Manhattan Skyline.

Thank you for reading. I hope you received some measure of entertainment and information.

As you read this, I am likely still on the road, traversing different communities and cultures, continuing my quest for psychological knowledge and insight. Knowledge that I hope to use for the benefit of myself and the world around me.

Whatever may happen, I hope all goes well with you. Perhaps we will inadvertently cross paths one day. Or, for some of you, cross paths again.

Vol II - New Content Guide

Vol II

Vol II

www.ingramcontent.com/pod-product-compliance
Lightning Source LLC
Chambersburg PA
CBHW071851090426
42811CB00004B/562